CW01637437

MICROWAVE COOKING

MICROWAVE COOKING

Margaret Fulton

HAMLYN
AUSTRALIA

This edition first Published in 1984 by Octopus
an imprint of Reed Consumer Books Limited
Michelin House
81 Fulham Road
London SW3 6RB

(c) 1983 Hennerwood Publications Limited

ISBN 0 7064 2138 8
Reprinted 1993

Produced by Mandarin Offset
Printed and Bound in Hong Kong

CONTENTS

NOTES

Standard cup and spoon measurements are used in all recipes.
1 cup = 250 ml
1 teaspoon = one 5 ml spoon
1 tablespoon = one 20 ml spoon
All spoon measurements are level.
Use standard 55 g eggs unless otherwise directed.
Metric and imperial measurements have been calculated separately. Use one set of measurements only as they are not exact equivalents.
Cooking times may vary slightly depending on the output of the microwave oven, the type and shape of container used and the temperature of the food.
The recipes in this book are timed for an oven with an output of 650 watts. Food will need to be cooked for a few minutes longer in an oven with a lower output.
Fresh herbs have been used in all recipes. If using dried herbs, halve the quantity given.

POWER LEVEL
START

INTRODUCTION

More and more modern cooks are cooking the microwave way. The first and best-known reason is that the microwave oven gives results in a fraction of the usual time. However, many microwave owners are almost as enthusiastic about its other benefits as about its speed.

Running costs are low, because the microwave energy concentrates on the food and not on the surrounding air and oven walls. The oven itself stays cool, so that cleanups are simply a matter of wiping spills and spatters with a damp cloth, and the kitchen is more comfortable in hot weather. Because it is a "cool" appliance, the microwave is of particular benefit to the disabled and the elderly.

The shorter cooking time results in retention of vitamins and minerals lost in conventional cooking. Since added liquids and fats are generally reduced or even eliminated and foods cook in their own juices, the results are more flavoursome, moister and better for you. Foods taste better with less or even no salt – another health benefit.

The microwave is brilliant for speedy reheating without loss of moisture or nutrients, and without giving the food a warmed-over taste . . . this makes it wonderfully useful for feeding a late-comer, for the tricky business of serving a main dish and all its accompaniments piping hot at the same moment, or for producing hot party food with magical ease.

WHAT ARE MICROWAVES?

Microwaves are a form of the electromagnetic energy which we all use every day in one way or another, for example when we watch television, listen to the radio, use an infra-red lamp or switch on a light bulb. It is the frequency at which the energy is used which determines its effect.

THE BASIC CONTROLS

The timer

Timing is an essential part of cooking with microwaves. The timer will automatically switch off the oven when the set time is up, and will ping, buzz or flash a light to show this. When you need to get to the food during cooking, open the door and the timed sequence will halt, while the microwaves will switch off instantly. Shut the door again, press the start button if necessary and the cooking time will continue without needing to be reset.

The on/off and start button

Many microwave ovens have an on/off button which switches on the power. Some ovens have a separate start button which starts the preset timed cooking sequence, though in some the sequence is started simply by closing the door.

The defrost control

Many ovens have a defrost control which may either reduce the wattage or pulse the energy on and off to thaw frozen food fast without cooking. The defrost control is also useful for cooking foods slowly after an initial period on maximum power.

Variable power control

This control enables you to use ¾ power, ½ power etc. for more gentle cooking of some foods.

PLACING YOUR MICROWAVE OVEN

A microwave oven needs only to be plugged in to a normal household power point and it is ready to use. It can go on a kitchen counter top, can be built in (providing it has adequate air circulation) or can be placed on a trolley so that it can be moved. You can take a microwave oven to the dining room table, out to the garden or the barbecue, to a weekend cottage or even on holidays.

Since air is drawn in by a fan to cool the magnetron, the air inlet grilles must not be blocked and the oven must not be placed where the air is likely to be hot, e.g. near a conventional stove top.

HERE'S HOW THE MICROWAVE OVEN WORKS

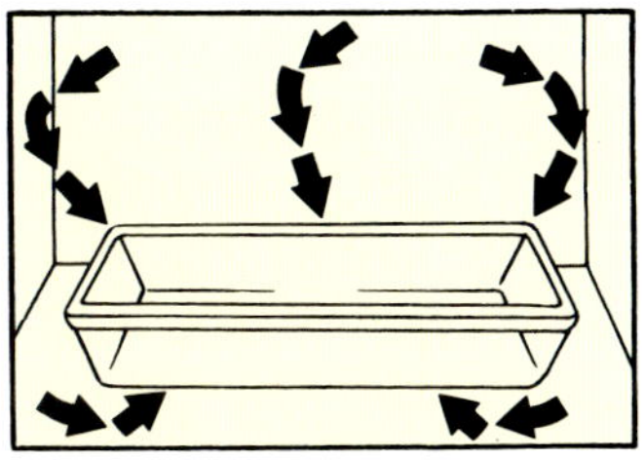

1

1. Reflected
Microwaves are short electromagnetic waves which are generated by the oven's magnetron (a vacuum tube which converts electrical energy into microwaves).

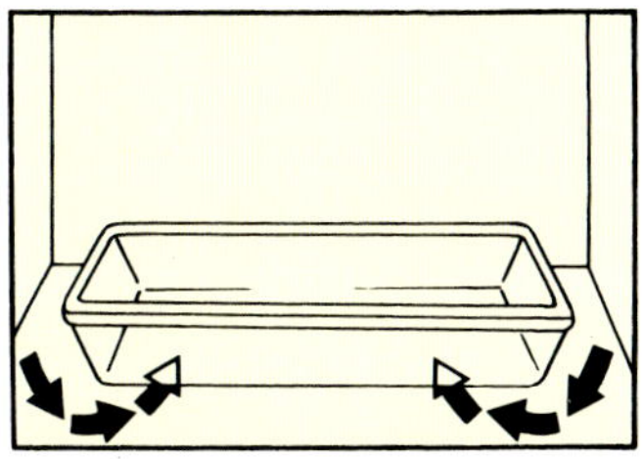

2

2. Transmitted
As microwaves enter the oven, they are reflected off the metal walls and transmitted through materials like glass, pottery, paper and plastic.

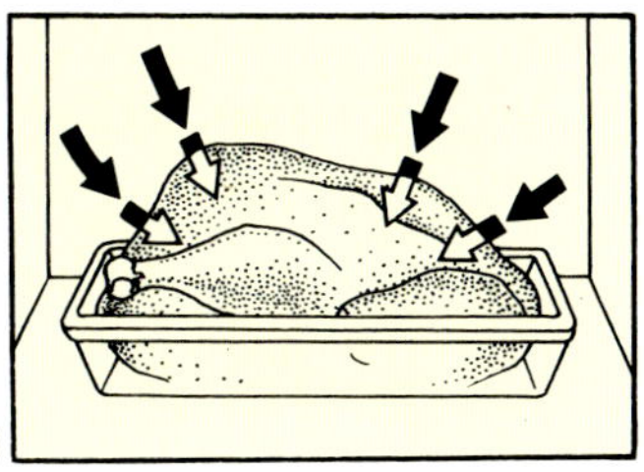

3

3. Absorbed
When they reach the food, they are attracted to its moisture content and absorbed. Microwaves vibrate at 2450 million times per second, causing friction of the molecules, which produces heat within the food so that it quickly "cooks itself". The microwaves penetrate immediately some 2.5-3 cm (1-1¼ inches) all round, and the heat generated within this layer is conducted through the food to cook the interior.

SAFETY

Microwave ovens are as safe as any other electrical appliance in the home. All microwave ovens for use and sale in Australia must be certified as meeting strict Government-applied safety standards which include a specified maximum emission level (thousands of times lower than that known to harm humans), three interlocks to prevent the unit operating with the door open and an intrusion-proof glass and metal door to keep the microwaves inside the oven.

MAINTENANCE

A microwave oven needs little or no maintenance if the manufacturer's instructions are followed. It is important that under no circumstances should anyone but a fully trained microwave serviceman dismantle the oven or try to carry out a repair.

The manufacturer's instruction book should always be referred to but in general:

- Any soil or spillage should be wiped clean with a damp cloth after use. If this is placed in the oven on Maximum for 30 seconds it becomes warm and easier to use. If the oven is very splattered, boil a cup of water with a little detergent in the oven for a minute or two, and the steam will make it easy to clean. If the oven needs freshening after cooking strong-smelling food, boil a cup of water with a spoonful of vanilla or a few slices of lemon in it for a few minutes, then wipe out the oven with a clean cloth.
- In particular, keep the door seal clean to ensure that it can do its job of sealing in the microwaves.
- Use liquid rather than powder cleaning agents, which may be abrasive and damage the oven.
- Do not operate the oven when it is empty. A cup of water placed in the cavity will absorb any microwaves if the oven is turned on accidentally.

COOKING UTENSILS

You can use many ordinary household containers for cooking in the microwave oven – ordinary plates, cups and bowls and also plastic and paper. There are a few exceptions, mainly metal or materials decorated with or containing metal, and a few plastics. Remember, however, that though microwaves will generally not damage utensils, the heat of the food may do so. For example, if you were to make caramel in a glass container, the sugar syrup would reach such a high temperature that it would crack the glass. For very high-temperature foods it is best to use specially manufactured pyroceram utensils such as Corningware.

Unless otherwise specified, choose wide, shallow containers rather than deep ones so that the microwaves can penetrate the food evenly.

Dish test

To decide whether a container is suitable for use in a microwave oven, test it as follows:

Fill a china or heat-resistant glass cup with water and place it in the container to be tested. Place both of them in the microwave oven and turn the setting to Maximum for 1½ minutes. If the water gets hot but the dish stays cool, it can be safely used in the microwave oven. If the water is cool and the dish is warm or hot, do not use. If the dish "sparks", simply turn the oven off immediately and don't use – the sparks indicate that there is metal in the dish and it is not safe.

Metals

Do not use metal utensils, china decorated with metal (e.g. gold rims), lead crystal or any material which contains metal such as the metal ties supplied with roasting bags (tie them with string).

Small pieces of aluminium foil may be used for part of the cooking time, to shield parts of the food that would otherwise overcook, such as turkey legs or chicken wings. So long as ⅔ of the food surface is exposed, the foil is smoothed on without wrinkles and the food does not touch the sides of the oven, this practice is acceptable in most microwave ovens. However, check with the manufacturer's instruction booklet if there is any doubt.

China and pottery utensils

All china and pottery is suitable, including teacups for individual portions and teapots for tea-making, providing that they contain no metal, are without metal decoration, are not cracked and do not have glued-on handles. Do not use antique china.

Wood and baskets

Food can be heated in wooden utensils or in a basket but leave these containers in the microwave for a few minutes only. Do not use baskets which have wire or staples.

Paper

Paper containers and plates are good for quick heating, but not for prolonged cooking as the containers must be able to withstand the heat and moisture produced by the food. Avoid paper utensils which have a wax finish as the heat of the food may melt it. Paper towels and greaseproof paper may be used to hold food for heating or to shield food such as a roast to prevent splattering. Paper napkins or towels are useful for warming bread or pastries. Place the food between 2 sheets of paper and heat on Maximum just until warm. Flour products will toughen if overheated.

Glass

Ovenproof glass and ordinary glass tumblers and dishes are suitable, but should not be used in recipes where the food may become hot enough to crack them. Do not cook food with a high proportion of fat or sugar in glass as it reaches very high temperatures. Pyroceram or glass-ceramic is the exception to this and is ideal for food at very high temperatures. Do not use glass with metal decoration or made from lead crystal.

Plastic

Plastic film and plastic freezer bags are useful for microwave cookery as they seal moisture in. When covering a dish with plastic film, seal it to the sides but leave some ease to accomodate the steam. In certain recipes, e.g. lasagne, the plastic film should be pricked or left open at one side so that it will not be sucked down on to the surface of the food. Do not use plastic film where it will come in contact with food containing a high proportion of fat or sugar, as the very high temperatures will break down the plastic.

Frozen vegetables can be cooked in the bag in which they were bought, so long as it is pierced first. Plastic containers such as icecream containers are suitable so long as the food cooked will not reach very high temperatures and so long as the container passes the dish test described.

Special browning utensils

Since microwave ovens do not get hot, foods do not

brown in the conventional way. This problem has been largely overcome by the introduction of special browning utensils, coated underneath with a metal oxide, which become very hot when preheated empty in the oven. When the food is placed in, it is browned by contact with the hot surface as in a frying pan, while the microwaves cook it through. These utensils cannot be used for conventional stove-top cooking.

Other special microwave utensils
There is a wide range of special utensils made for use in microwave ovens. They include ridged roasting racks which hold the meat out of the juices, muffin pans which can also hold eggs for poaching, cake pans, biscuit trays etc. One or two such pieces will probably prove useful for your microwave cooking, but don't rush into buying them. Use ordinary household utensils at first (an upturned plate can substitute for a roasting rack, cups or ramekins for muffin pans, souffle dishes or casseroles for cake pans, a large plate or the glass turntable of the microwave oven for biscuit trays). When you know how you are going to use your microwave most, you will know which special utensils will be worth their price and their space in your kitchen.

Utensil and cooking advice
It is best to choose a container in which the food may be spread evenly and be evenly exposed to the action of the microwaves. Round dishes give better results than square ones and shallow dishes are better than deep ones. A utensil which is narrower at one end will cook the food more quickly in the narrow area.

Avoid cooking cakes in square or oblong containers, as the corners may overcook and become dry. Ring-shaped utensils will frequently give a better result as the centre of a cake is the slowest part to cook.

When heating liquids, choose a container large enough to avoid boiling over. Glasses should be strong enough to withstand the temperature of the heated liquid. When thawing liquid-based foods, such as soups, place the frozen block in a tight-fitting container so the thawed liquid is retained close to the frozen block.

Cover foods which need to cook by moisture, e.g. stews, soups, fish, peeled fruit and vegetables. Plates, casserole lids and plastic film can be used as covers.

Do not cover foods which are intended to be "dry", e.g. cakes, pastry, fruit and vegetables in skins and bread products. Roasts and other meats cooked on a browning utensil may be covered with paper towels to prevent spattering while allowing moisture to escape.

MICROWAVE TECHNIQUES

Microwave cooking is easy, but uses some techniques which are different from those of conventional cooking. You will soon become familiar with them.

Timing
Timing plays a much more important part in the cooking results obtained from a microwave oven than in conventional cooking. It is wise to undercook, check and return the food to the oven if necessary to continue cooking. Overcooking or heating will dehydrate the food and make it tough or hard.

The cooking time needed varies with the quantity of food being cooked at one time. For example one jacket potato may take 5 minutes to cook but two take 8 minutes. This is simply because the level of microwave energy remains the same and has to be distributed among an increased quantity of food.

The power of your oven also affects cooking time. The recipes in this book are based on a 650-watt oven. Ovens with less power may need additional time, as in the following chart:

600-650 Watts	500-600 Watts	400-500 Watts
15 sec.	17 sec.	20 sec.
30 sec.	35 sec.	41 sec.
1 min.	1 min. 9 sec.	1 min. 21 sec.
2 min.	2 min. 22 sec.	2 min. 42 sec.
3 min.	3 min. 27 sec.	4 min. 3 sec.
4 min.	4 min. 36 sec.	5 min. 24 sec.
5 min.	5 min. 45 sec.	6 min. 45 sec.
10 min.	11 min. 30 sec.	13 min. 30 sec.
15 min.	17 min. 15 sec.	20 min. 15 sec.
20 min.	23 min.	27 min.
25 min.	25 min. 45 sec.	33 min. 45 sec.
30 min.	34 min. 30 sec.	40 min. 30 sec.

Positioning food for cooking
Since the lowest activity of microwave energy is next to the walls, in the corners and in the absolute centre of the oven, it is best to place a single item off-centre, unless otherwise directed by the manufacturer. Because food will cook more around the outside edge of the dish, arrange it with heavier parts to the outside. For example, chicken drumsticks or fish steaks should be placed with the thick end outward and the thinner part toward the centre of the dish. Arrange broccoli with the stalk outward and the flower inside. When reheating a meal on a plate, place the larger and denser foods such as potatoes or pumpkin round the outside, with peas or beans and meat toward the centre (cover the plate with plastic film to keep food moist).

When cooking more than one container or item of food, follow these diagrams:

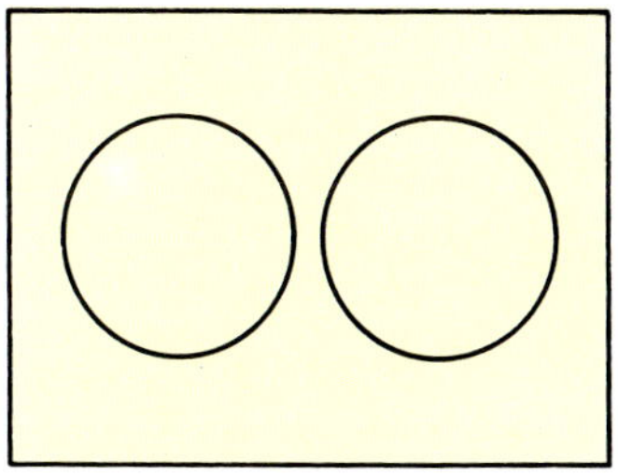
If cooking two or more items, set at least one inch apart.

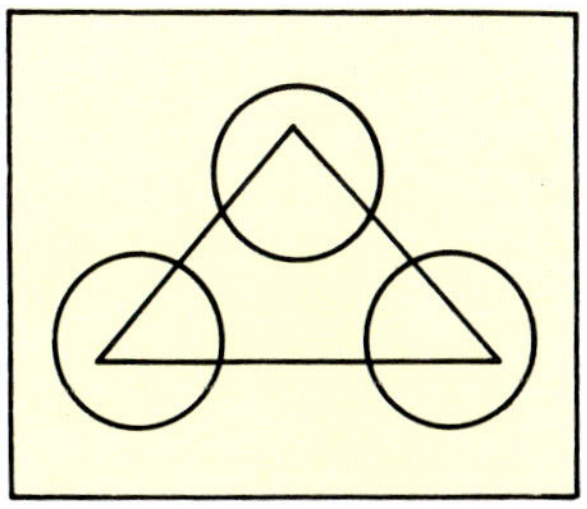
Three items, set in the angles of an imaginary triangle.

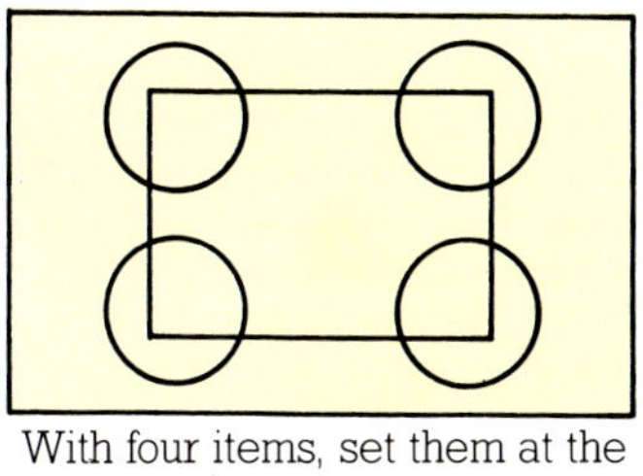
With four items, set them at the corners of a square.

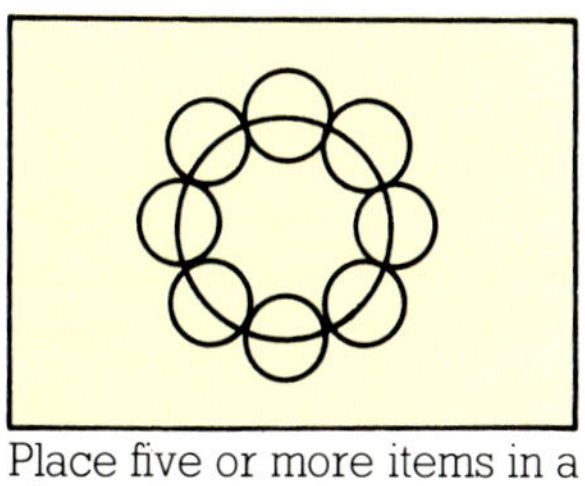
Place five or more items in a circle, leaving the centre free.

Browning food
When cooked conventionally, the outer layer of food browns from the oven heat. The method by which microwaves cook, providing heat within the food by molecular friction, does not brown the outside. Large joints with a high fat content or a whole turkey will brown somewhat because their longer cooking times allow the outer fat to reach temperatures at which it changes colour, in the same way that butter will brown if heated sufficiently in a microwave oven. However, browning will be less than in a conventional oven. Poultry usually looks better if rubbed before cooking with soy, teriyaki or barbecue sauce or brushed with melted butter and paprika or tomato paste and brown sugar thinned with a little water, or other glazes which will give colour. A sprinkle of paprika will give a "browned" look to cheese topping, while buttered breadcrumbs or coconut toppings contain enough fat to brown naturally when heated.

Foods can also be browned, after microwave cooking, under a preheated conventional grill or in a frying pan, or a roast can be placed in a preheated conventional oven to dry and crisp the outer surface.

Some modern microwave ovens have a built-in browning element, or combine convection cooking (cooking by fan-forced conventional heat) with microwave cooking. Follow the manufacturer's directions for cooking in these particular ovens.

Microwave browning dishes are ideal for sausages, steaks, chops, hamburgers, pikelets, toasted sandwiches and roasts. Preheat the dish according to the manufacturer's instructions and place the food in, "presentation" side (the side which will show when served) downward. Brush fatless meats (such as skinned poultry or fish) with oil or butter before placing in, to assist browning. Turn food during cooking as directed in recipe. Cover roasts and other food which may spatter with paper towels. Choose lean meat or trim off excess fat.

Stirring
The outer areas of food are getting more exposure to microwave energy while cooking, so foods such as casseroles or soups should be stirred once or twice, spooning the outside toward the centre so that contents cook evenly. Also stir or pour liquids such as thick soups or sauces just before reheating, to break up the surface film and prevent pressure build-up and eruption.

In the case of sauces, stirring will help to prevent lumps from forming.

Rearranging
Microwave energy is not distributed evenly thoughout the oven so food in one part may cook more quickly than food in another part. By changing the position of food part way through cooking, this can be evened out. If your oven has a turntable, rearranging may not be necessary as the turntable changes the relative positions of the food constantly.

Turning round
Turning round the container, for example when cooking a cake, or turning round items such as baked apples evens out the differences in microwave energy the food is receiving from different directions.

Turning over
Many foods are irregular in shape so exposure will vary across the food. By turning over, a more even cooking result can be achieved.

Standing, covered, after cooking
After cooking, foods may be left to stand for a specified number of minutes. This standing time, or carry-on cooking time, is an integral part of microwave cooking. The energy generated within the food is so intense that cooking continues after it is removed from the oven. The food will remain hot, in fact some foods increase in temperature while standing. Foods are usually covered during this time to help retain heat. Lids and plastic wrap hold in moisture and are used when this is beneficial. Paper towels, greaseproof paper or a loose tent of foil, shiny side inward, over a joint or poultry holds in heat without steaming the food.

USING THE RECIPES

The recipes in this book are designed for an oven with a maximum output of 650 watts. If you have an oven with a lower output you will find it necessary to increase times slightly (see chart under "Microwave Techniques; Timing" on page 9).

All the food used in the recipes was at room temperature. Should food be used from the refrigerator or quantities increase, then a slightly longer cooking time may be required. Cooking times may also, of course, vary according to the way you like your food. Where a recipe says, for example, "Cook 4-6 minutes", check at the earlier time then return to the oven for more cooking if needed.

All food is cooked uncovered unless otherwise stated in the recipes.

SOUPS

Comforting home-made soup is a simple proposition with a microwave. It is usually made using just one large bowl, which may be the soup tureen itself so long as it is wide rather than narrow and deep. It's quick, wonderfully fresh-tasting and colourful since vegetables retain their colour when cooked in this way.

EGGS AND CHEESE

Always remove egg dishes from the microwave before they look completely cooked, then stand for a minute or two before serving. Prick yolks before cooking to prevent bursting. Most forms of eggs can be cooked but eggs in shells cannot be cooked without bursting unless great care is taken, and I do not advise attempting this.

When adding eggs to sauces, count cooking in seconds rather than minutes and check frequently to avoid overcooking. Delicate dishes such as egg custards are best cooked on a lower setting or with the dish standing in another dish of water, as this makes cooking more gentle. Hard-boiled eggs added to a dish which is then microwaved can go tough and rubbery but they can be used so long as cooking is brief.

Grated or sliced cheese melts very quickly and if overcooked will become stringy, so it must be added only right toward the end of cooking time. When adding cheese to hot sauces, it is not usually necessary to cook the sauce any further. Simply stir the cheese into the sauce until it melts.

MEAT

Meat frequently cooks with less shrinkage in the microwave oven than in a conventional one.

If a recipe calls for a meat dish to be partly cooked on

Defrost or Medium setting, and your microwave oven has only one (Maximum) setting, it is best to choose a more tender cut of meat than that specified in the recipe. Steak sold as "barbecue steak" is suitable for casseroling, but cheaper and tougher cuts of meat will not normally give good results if they cannot be cooked more slowly than at the Maximum setting. If cooking entirely on Maximum, allow 3-4 minutes per 500 g (1 lb) of cubed meat, and allow the same standing time as that given in the recipe.

FISH

Fish is moister and more flavoursome when cooked in a microwave oven. Cooking times are short; remember that it is better to undercook than to overcook – check after standing time and return fish to the oven for a few moments if necessary.

Fish fillets or steaks, dusted with flour if desired, may be sauteed and crumbed fish may be shallow-fried, in a little butter, oil or a mixture of these in a preheated browning dish.

Note: Do not attempt to deep-fry in a microwave oven.

Always cover fish while cooking as it can spatter suddenly. Use a lid of plastic film for moist cooking, a paper towel for cooking in a browning dish.

RICE, PULSES AND PASTA

Rice cooks beautifully in the microwave, especially by the absorption method. Pasta is also very successful, though as it requires a large quantity of water, it is quicker and more economical to boil this in a kettle rather than in the microwave. It is essential that rice and pasta be left to stand, covered, for some minutes after the cooking time and this can be useful if a sauce is being prepared. For the best results a very large, covered container should be used. The addition of a little oil will prevent the water from boiling over.

If making a rice milk pudding, it is best to use a lower setting and an extra large container. As there is no external heat, the top of the pudding will not brown to the same degree as in conventional cooking. If a fairly thick rice pudding is desired, remove the cover of the dish ¾ of the way through cooking.

DEFROSTING can be done in a microwave oven which does not have a defrost cycle. Allow 2 minutes/500 g (1 lb) on full power and add to that 2 minutes/500 g (1 lb) resting time. Stand after defrosting to finish the process.

DEFROSTING USING MAXIMUM/FULL POWER

	Power on	Rest	Standing time at completion of defrosting and resting
Small or flat frozen foods	1-2 minutes	1-2 minutes	1-2 minutes
Large or compact frozen foods	5 minutes	5 minutes	5 minutes

The food **must be** rotated and corners and warm areas shielded with foil during the defrosting process, or the outer edges will start to cook.

The advice given by manufacturers on cooking dried beans, peas and lentils in the microwave is varied, and it is advisable to check the manufacturer's instruction book for guidance as to the method, time and setting required. Beans and chick peas, which need long, slow cooking, may be harder than usual and your own taste will decide whether this is acceptable. Lentils are more successful since they do not normally require lengthy slow cooking. The microwave is, however, very useful for performing the preliminary soaking of beans and peas quickly and easily, rather than overnight (see "Making the Most of Your Microwave", pages 14 and 15).

DEFROSTING POULTRY & LARGE CUTS OF MEAT

Meat

Cuts of meat	Weight	Time in mins. on Defrost/⅓ power	Standing Time in mins.
Whole fillet of beef	1-1.25 kg/ 2-3 lb	15-20	20
Rolled Roast	1.5 kg/3 lb	30	30
Rump Roast	1.5-2 kg/ 3-4 lb	25-35	30
Leg of Lamb	2 kg/4 lb	30-35	30
Leg of Pork	2-2.5 kg/ 4-5 lb	35-45	40
Poultry			
Chickens, whole per	500 g/1 lb	7-10	30
Chicken pieces (wings, drumsticks, thighs) – separate pieces during defrosting	500 g/1 lb	4-8	10-15
Chicken breasts, whole	500 g/1 lb	5-8	15-20
Chicken livers – separate during defrosting	500 g/1 lb	4-8	10
Turkey, whole per	500 g/1 lb	5-9	45-60
Ducks, whole per	500 g/1 lb	7-10	30

DEFROSTING FISH/SEAFOOD

Fish/Seafood	Weight	Time in mins. on Defrost/⅓ power (covered)	Standing Time in mins. (covered)
Frozen fillets – as fillets defrost remove them from the frozen portion to prevent cooking	500 g/1 lb	10-12	5
Whole fish	750 g-1 kg/ 1½-2 lb	13-15	15
Fish cutlets or steaks 2.5 cm/1 inch thick	500 g/1 lb	5-6	5
Prawns/scallops	250 g/8 oz 500 g/1 lb	3-4 5-6	3-4 5-6
Lobster tails	250 g/8 oz	6-7	6-7

Note: Cover fish fillets, steaks and cutlets with paper towels while defrosting.

COOKING SMALL CUTS OF MEAT

Cut, Type and Weight of Meat	Special Points	Approx. Cooking Time in mins Max/Full Power	Standing Time in mins. (covered)
Minced Beef, 500 g/1 lb	Covered in a bowl or uncovered in a browning casserole	5	2
Steak-Fillet, Scotch Fillet, Rump, 250 g/8 oz	Best cooked in a browning dish	3-4	2
Lamb or Pork Chops, 155 g/5 oz each	Chops should be well-trimmed of fat	6	2
Lamb or Veal Cutlets, (4), 500 g/1 lb		5-6	2
Veal or Pork Schnitzel, 500 g/1 lb	Dip crumbed schnitzel in melted butter. Cook on a preheated browning dish turning once	4-5	2
Bacon Rashers, 60-90 g/2-3 oz each	Cook on paper towels or a rack	¾-1	2
Ham Steaks (cooked), 375 g packet of 4	Arrange on a plate and cover, or brush steaks with oil or melted butter and cook on a preheated browning dish turning once.	1½-2½	2
Lambs' Fry, 500 g/1 lb, trimmed	Slice thinly	6	2
Lambs' Kidneys (4), 250 g/8 oz	Cook covered on a plate **or** on a preheated browning dish	2-2½	2
Lambs' Brains, 3 sets	Soak, rinse, trim and blanch. Slit in half. Dust with seasoned flour. Coat with melted butter, cook on a preheated browning dish turning once	3-4	2

COOKING FISH/SEAFOOD

Fish/Seafood	Weight	Time in mins. on Max/Full Power (covered)	Standing Time in mins. (covered)
Fillets	500 g/1 lb 1 kg/2 lb	3-4 6-7	2 2-3
Whole fish	750 g-1 kg/ 1½ lb-2 lb	7-10	3-4
Fish cutlets or steaks 2.5 cm/1 inch thick	500 g/1 lb 1 kg/2 lb	4-5 7-8	2 3
Prawns	250 g/8 oz 500 g/1 lb	3-4 5-7	2 3
		Time in mins. on Medium-High/¾ Power	
Scallops/ Oysters	250 g/8 oz 500 g/1 lb	5-6 8-9	2 3
Lobsters	500 g/1 lb 750 g-1 kg/ 1½-2 lb	7-8 9-12	3 4
Smoked fish (in freezer bag)	500 g/1 lb	5	3-4

COOKING POULTRY & LARGE CUTS OF MEAT

Poultry/cut of meat per 500 g/1 lb	Approx. Cooking Time in mins. Max/Full Power	Max/Full Power for 10 mins.	Total Standing Time in mins. (covered)
		Then Medium-High/ ¾ Power	
Roast Beef, (uncovered)			
rare	5-7	8-9	20
medium	7-8	9-10	
well-done	8-10	11-12	
Roast Lamb (uncovered)	7-9	10-11	20
Roast Pork (uncovered)	9-10	11-12	20
Roast Veal (uncovered)	7-9	10-11	20
Hams (pre-cooked), covered or uncovered	6-7	8-9	20
Chickens, whole roast	6-7	8-9	15-20
		or Max/Full Power for 10 mins, then Medium/ ½ power	
Corned Silverside, (covered)	9-11	20	15
Pickled Pork, (covered)	9-11	20	15
Pickled Smoked Tongues, (covered)	9-11	20	15
Ducks/duckling roast, (uncovered)	6-7	7-9	15-20
Turkeys, small roast, (uncovered)	6-7	12-15	30
Turkeys, large over No.45, (4.5 kg/10 lb)	not recommended		

COOKING FROZEN VEGETABLES

Frozen Vegetable	Weight or volume	Approx. Cooking Time in mins. Maximum/ Full Power	Standing Time
Beans, Green	1 cup 500 g/1 lb	2 10-12	1 3-4
Broccoli	500 g/1 lb	5-6	3
Brussels Sprouts	500 g/1 lb	5-6	3
Carrots	500 g/1 lb	5-6	3
Cauliflower	500 g/1 lb	5-6	3
Corn on the Cob	2 cobs 1 cup niblets 500 g niblets	6-8 2 4-6	3 1 3
Peas, Green	500 g/1 lb	4-6	3
Spinach, leaf or chopped	500 g/1 lb	5-6	3
Vegetables, mixed	1 cup 500 g/1 lb	2 4-6	1 3

COOKING FRESH VEGETABLES

Fresh Vegetable and Weight	Preparation	Water to be added	Approx. Cooking Time in mins. Maximum/Full Power	Standing Time in mins.
Asparagus, 500 g/1 lb	Wash and trim	2 tablespoons	4-5	2-4
Artichokes, 4 medium	Wash and trim	½ cup	10-20	"
Beetroot, 500 g/1 lb	Wash, skin and cut in half	None	7-8	"
Broad beans, 500 g/1 lb	Remove from pods and wash	2 tablespoons	7-10	"
Broccoli, 250 g/8 oz	Prepare, slice into spears	3 tablespoons	4-5	"
Brussels Sprouts, 250 g/8 oz	Trim	3-4 tablespoons	7-8	"
Cabbage, 500 g/1 lb	Trim and shred	3 tablespoons	7-8	"
Carrots, 250 g/8 oz	Scrape and slice	2 tablespoons	6-7	"
Cauliflower, 500 g/1 lb	Trim and cut into florets	4 tablespoons	9-10	"
Celery, 1 bunch	Trim and dice	½ cup	10-13	"
Corn on the Cob (2)	Trim and wash	4 tablespoons	4-6	"
Eggplant, 500 g/1 lb	Peel and dice	2 tablespoons	5-6	"
Green Beans, 250 g/8 oz	String and slice	4 tablespoons	4	"
Leeks, 500 g/1 lb	Trim and slice	3 tablespoons	7-9	"
Mushrooms, button, 125 g/4 oz	Wipe, leave whole	2 tablespoons	2½-3	"
Onions, diced, 1 medium, 100 g/3½ oz	Peel and dice	None	4-6	"
Onions, whole, approx. 4 medium, 500 g/1 lb	Peel and cut a cross in root end	2 tablespoons	4-6	"
Parsnips, 500 g/1 lb	Peel and slice	3 tablespoons	6-8	"
Peas, 250 g/8 oz	Remove from pods and wash	3 tablespoons	6-8	"
Potatoes, boiled 500 g/1 lb	Peel and cut into even-size pieces	3 tablespoons	6-7	"
Potatoes, jacket (2), 250-300 g/8-10 oz	Scrub and prick well	None	9	"
Pumpkin, 500 g/1 lb	Peel and cut in chunks	2 tablespoons	5-7	"
Silverbeet, 1 bunch, 1 kg/2 lb	Wash and shred	None	5-7	"
Spinach, 250 g/8 oz	Wash and shred	None	6-8	"
Swede Turnips, 250 g/8 oz	Peel and dice	None	6-8	"
Sweet Potatoes, whole, 500 g/1 lb	Wash and prick	None Cook on paper towel	7-9	"
sliced, 500 g/1 lb	Wash, peel and slice	2 tablespoons	6-7	"
Tomatoes, 250 g/8 oz	Slice	None	2-3	"
Turnips, white, 250 g/8 oz	Peel and dice	2 tablespoons	6-7	"
Zucchini, 500 g/1 lb	Trim and slice	None	4-6	"

SPECIAL POINTS FOR ALL VEGETABLES: Place vegetables in a bowl. Add required amount of water. Cook covered. Leave to stand, covered, for 2 minutes, after cooking or for the time stated in the actual recipe, strain and season to taste.

Vegetables may also be cooked in a freezer bag using no water. Tie and prick the bag and cook the vegetables in their own juices. Reduce time a little. **No** salt is necessary as the vegetables retain their natural flavour. Take care when opening as steam will be released.

PUDDINGS AND CAKES

The microwave makes it easy to produce the lovely old-fashioned puddings that everyone loves but may seem rather a lot of trouble to cook by conventional means.

Steamed puddings cook in their own moisture, and this does away with the inconvenience of steaming pans on a stove and the ever constant need to replenish water. Fruit is cooked to perfection in little or no water and retains both shape and vivid colours, and the flavour of the cooked product is much closer to that of the fresh uncooked fruit.

Pastry is less successful and only a shortcrust pastry tart shell or suet pudding are likely to be acceptable. The short crust will be paler than usual, but crisp and tender. Crumb crusts are very successful.

Cooking cakes in the microwave is an area where much will depend on the recipe and the expectations of the cook. Cakes will not brown, so unless the mixture is a coloured one such as chocolate, some form of decoration will be needed to give eye appeal. Icing and whipped cream coverings also help to retain moisture, an important consideration since microwave cakes tend to dry out quickly. Freezing leftover cake or a cake made ahead of time will prevent drying out, and portions of cake reheat very successfully in the microwave.

Do not grease or flour containers in which cakes are cooked in a microwave. Greasing is not only unnecessary but undesirable since it tends to cause a dense layer at the bottom of the cake. Flouring leaves an unattractive film on the outside of the cake. Line the base of the container with a piece of paper towel to facilitate turning out and also to absorb moisture which may collect at the bottom.

DRINKS AND PRESERVES

The microwave oven is ideal for heating up and making hot drinks right in the cups and tea in the teapot (see "Making the Most of Your Microwave", on the right).

Jams and chutneys cooked in the microwave are fresh-flavoured and more colourful than those cooked conventionally. The microwave is ideal for making a few pots of preserves because there is no risk of scorching. However, if making very large quantities of preserves, you may find it cheaper and more convenient to use the conventional methods.

When making jam and chutney in the microwave it is important to use a very large container to avoid any boiling over, to use a cloth when handling the container since the high temperature of the contents will make it hot, and never to leave a sugar or confectionery thermometer in the microwave while cooking.

SAUCES

Once you have made sauces in the microwave you may never want to make them conventionally again. You can often make the sauce in the serving bowl, often all the ingredients can be blended together in one step before cooking, lumpy sauces are less likely and the sauce cannot scorch or stick. A further advantage is the speed and convenience of reheating sauces, so many can be made in advance.

The choice of utensils is important to successful sauce-making in the microwave. Do invest in a wire whisk if you don't already own one, it is much the best implement for stirring a sauce to smoothness. Choose a bowl rather than a jug for cooking, since a straight-sided container creates a chimney effect and a thickened liquid will boil right up and over.

USING YOUR MICROWAVE

Cooking the microwave way is a skill like any other. Once you've developed it, you will make full and confident use of your microwave oven. Read your manufacturer's instruction booklet thoroughly and become familiar with the operation and features of your oven model. Classes in microwave cooking, offered by some manufacturers and also by many Technical Colleges, can be a great help in becoming adept at microwave procedures. Follow recipes carefully, making notes of any points and variations that will help to produce food to your individual taste the next time you make that recipe or a similar one in your particular model. Don't forget it's always better to undercook than overcook, microwaving is so quick that you can always return a dish to the oven for a little extra cooking time.

Do remember to think of your microwave as a helpful performer of many little kitchen tasks, as well as an appliance for cooking whole dishes. In any conventional recipe, look for steps you can do with the microwave to save time and cleaning up, such as scalding milk, melting chocolate or softening butter. On the right you will find "Making the Most of Your Microwave", a list of many little tasks your microwave can do to help even when you're cooking with a conventional stove. In later chapters there are planned menus, together with an "order of cooking". These will give you guidance to take you through all the stages of producing delicious meals from your microwave oven.

MAKING THE MOST OF YOUR MICROWAVE

Your microwave oven can save you time, money and cleaning up with many little jobs in the kitchen. Use it in these ways:

Soften butter or cream cheese. Unwrap, cut into pieces and place round a plate. Microwave on Medium-Low, turning plate every 15 seconds, or on Maximum, turning every 5 seconds. If butter or cheese begins to melt, remove and stand until evenly softened.

Melt or brown butter. 60 g (2 oz) takes 45-60 seconds on Maximum to melt, 2-3 minutes to brown.

Clarify butter. Melt in a shallow dish until foaming. Skim off foam, leave to settle 1-2 minutes then pour or spoon off clear liquid. Residue can be used to flavour vegetables.

Warm butter and sugar to be creamed for a cake, together in the mixing bowl, on Maximum for 15-30 seconds.

Warm plates by sprinkling with water, stacking on a microwave rack or placing on oven shelf and heating on Maximum for 1 minute.

Melt chocolate. Break into pieces, place round a small dish and heat uncovered, checking every minute, until it can be stirred. Note that chocolate holds its shape until stirred. 60 g (2 oz) takes about 3½ minutes on Maximum.

Place chocolate-covered after-dinner mints on cupcakes or biscuits, arrange in a circle on a plate and microwave on Maximum until chocolate is glossy. Spread softened mint and cool.

Make croutons. Melt 30 g (1 oz) butter in a shallow dish, add 2 cups cubed bread and toss. Spread out and heat, stirring several times, on Maximum for 4-5 minutes or until crisp and golden.

Blanch almonds. Place 1 cup hot water in a small casserole, heat on Maximum until boiling. Add 1 cup shelled almonds, spread out and heat uncovered on Maximum for 1 minute. Drain, slip skins off and spread on paper towels to dry.

Toast almonds. Melt 1 tablespoon butter in a pie plate, toss with ½ cup blanched whole almonds or ¼ cup slivered or flaked almonds. Heat on Maximum, stirring every 2 minutes, until light golden brown (almonds will darken further after removing from oven). Stand 5 minutes.

Toast sesame seeds. Melt 1 tablespoon butter in a cup, stir in 3 tablespoons sesame seeds and heat on Maximum, stirring every minute, until light golden brown (seeds will darken further after removing from oven). Stand 2-3 minutes and drain on a paper towel.

"Soak" burghul for tabbouli. Cover ½ cup burghul with cold water, cover and microwave on Medium for 5 minutes. Stand, covered, 5 minutes. Squeeze and dry on a teatowel as usual.

Soften hard brown sugar. Microwave, covered, with an

apple slice for 30-60 seconds, checking every 15 seconds. Stand, covered, for 5 minutes. If sugar begins to melt, remove from oven and let stand to complete softening.

Dry herbs or lavender. Strip leaves from stems and spread in a single layer on paper towels on a plate. Time varies with individual herbs but averages about 4 minutes on Maximum. Crumble, then store in airtight containers.

Freshen slightly stale bread and cake. Wrap 2 slices in a paper towel and heat about 15 seconds until just warm, not hot. Use immediately.

Warm baby bottles and baby food in its glass jar. Allow 45 seconds and upward for bottles, depending on quantity and starting temperature. Remove metal lids from jars and heat 15-30 seconds. Stand a few minutes and check temperature before feeding baby.

Dry grated orange and lemon peel to use in recipes, decorate iced cakes, sprinkle on cooked vegetables, fish or chicken. Sprinkle 2 tablespoons grated peel in a single layer on a plate and microwave on Maximum, turning plate and lifting and tossing peel with fingers every minute, for 2-4 minutes or until dry to the touch. Stand uncovered 2 hours or until completely dry and brittle. Store in a screwtop jar. ½ teaspoon dried peel is equivalent to 1 teaspoon grated fresh peel.

Peel tomatoes or peaches. Place 4 cups hot water in a large heatproof bowl, cover with plastic film, microwave on Maximum until boiling. Add 1-3 fruits (with microwave off), count to 10, remove fruit to a bowl of cold water. For additional fruit, return water to boiling and repeat. Nick skins with a pointed knife and peel off.

Put ½ cup of Choc-bits in a bowl, microwave on Maximum 2-3 minutes until melted, stir in ½ cup sour cream. Use to frost sides and top of a 23 cm (9 in) round cake. Refrigerate cake after frosting.

Place 15 g (½ oz) of chopped chocolate in the corner of a small plastic bag. Leave the bag open. Microwave on Maximum for 2 minutes, snip the corner and use to decorate or write on an iced cake.

For a child's treat, top a biscuit with a marshmallow and a few Choc-bits, microwave on Maximum until marshmallow begins to puff then press another biscuit on top.

Warm honey or golden syrup for easier measuring or to serve with pancakes or waffles. Microwave on Maximum for 30-45 seconds (if warming it in its jar, remove metal top first). Crystallised honey and refrigerated oils and salad dressings can be liquefied in the same way.

Warm jam for a quick and colourful meat glaze or dessert sauce. Microwave until melted, stirring every minute, then sieve if desired.

Toast shelled nuts or dried seeds, spread out on a plate, heat on Maximum for 4-5 minutes per cupful.

Make dried breadcrumbs. Place fresh breadcrumbs in a shallow dish and heat on Maximum, stirring frequently, for 4-5 minutes per cupful.

Make browned crumbs to top a vegetable or savoury dish. Melt 30 g (1 oz) butter, toss with 1½ cups dried crumbs, heat on Maximum, stirring frequently, until browned. For herbed crumbs, add a tablespoon chopped herbs to the melted butter.

Warm citrus fruits to obtain more juice. Heat on Maximum for 15-30 seconds and stand 3 minutes before squeezing.

Cook rolled oats for 1, in the serving bowl. Place ¼ cup quick-cooking oats, ½ cup water and a pinch of salt in the bowl. Cook uncovered 1¼ minutes, stir, cover and stand a few minutes before serving. May be cooked ahead and reheated.

Warm bread rolls or croissants in their napkin-lined basket for 30-60 seconds, just until warm, not hot, immediately before serving.

Scald milk. Measure in a heatproof measuring jug and microwave uncovered on Maximum, watching, just until bubbles form round edge. Open door immediately to switch off power and prevent boiling over. Milk for hot drinks, or a mug of soup, can be heated in the same way. Stir or pour soup immediately before heating to break surface film and prevent spitting.

Make a cup of tea, coffee or instant soup. Fill cups or mugs with cold water and heat uncovered on Maximum. 1 cup takes about 1 minute, 2 cups take 3½ minutes. Add tea bag, instant coffee or sachet of soup mix. You can also make tea in the teapot. Fill with water, bring to the boil and add tea. Be sure teapot does not have any metal parts or a glued-on handle.

Make fast, delicious "roast" potatoes. For tender potatoes with a light, crisp outside, peel them, cut into pieces and cook, covered, with 3 tablespoons water for 6 minutes (for 500 g/1 lb) or until tender. Drain, dry with a cloth and score surface with a fork. Brush with oil and grill under a preheated conventional griller, turning until golden. For potatoes with a crunchy crust, peel and cut into pieces then cook uncovered for 6 minutes (for 500 g/1 lb). The potatoes will have a thick, dry outside layer. Brush with oil and grill under a preheated conventional griller, turning until golden.

Soften pumpkin to make it easier to cut, by microwaving on Maximum for 1½ minutes or until just warm.

Make fried bread. Brush with melted butter mixed with a little paprika and bake on a microwave rack or paper towels, on Maximum for 2-3 minutes or until crisp. Turn bread once.

Reconstitute dried apples, pears, peaches etc. Cover with water, heat on High 6-8 minutes. Stand, covered, 5 minutes.

Plump raisins or prunes. Add 1-3 teaspoons water, tea, orange juice or port, cover and microwave on Maximum for 30-45 seconds. Stand, covered, for 2-3 minutes and drain if necessary.

Warm brandy or other spirits for flaming. Heat on Maximum 30 seconds, light and pour over food.

Soften hard icecream for serving. Warm on Maximum 15-30 seconds, stand 2-3 minutes. If necessary, heat another few seconds.

Cook hot dogs in their rolls. Place a frankfurt in a lightly-buttered roll and wrap in a paper towel. Microwave for 45 seconds-1¼ minutes on Maximum until buns are warm. Frankfurt will be hot because of its greater moisture content.

Pre-soak dried beans and peas, quickly and easily. Place 250 g (8 oz) beans or peas with 4 cups water in a large casserole or bowl and cover tightly. Heat on Maximum for 4-5 minutes or until boiling. Stand, covered, 1 hour.

Remember to read the labels on prepared and processed foods. Many have instructions for microwaving.

Potato and onion soup; Lentil and orange soup

POTATO & ONION SOUP

Serves 4 Cooking time: about 21 minutes
Microwave setting: Maximum (Full)

2 large onions, peeled and finely chopped
750 g (1½ lb) potatoes, peeled and thinly sliced
¼ teaspoon grated nutmeg
2½ cups milk
1½ cups hot beef stock
salt
freshly ground black pepper
2 teaspoons snipped chives

Place the onions and potatoes in a large bowl, cover and cook for 13 minutes, stirring halfway through cooking.

Stir in the nutmeg and milk. Cover and cook for 4½ minutes, stirring halfway through cooking.

Stir in the beef stock and salt and pepper to taste. Puree in a blender or rub through a sieve, then return to the bowl and reheat 3-4 minutes.

Serve sprinkled with chives.

LENTIL & ORANGE SOUP

Serves 4 Cooking time: 27 minutes
Microwave setting: Maximum (Full)

30 g (1 oz) butter
½ cup red lentils
1 onion, peeled and finely chopped
1 celery stick, finely sliced
½ medium carrot, peeled and grated
1 teaspoon ground cumin
3½ cups hot chicken stock
½ cup orange juice
grated rind of ½ orange
bay leaf
freshly ground black pepper
salt
slivered orange rind

Place the butter and lentils in a large bowl. Cover and cook for 2 minutes, stirring halfway through.

Stir in the onion, celery, carrot and cumin. Cover and cook for 7 minutes, stirring halfway through.

Stir in 2½ cups of the hot stock with the orange juice, grated rind, bay leaf and pepper. Cover and cook for 10 minutes, stirring halfway through.

Remove the bay leaf and stir in the remaining hot stock. Cool slightly.

Pour the soup into a blender and blend.

Return to the bowl and reheat for 8 minutes.

Season with salt and garnish with slivered rind.

SOUPS

COUNTRY VEGETABLE SOUP

Serves 4-6 Cooking time: about 20 minutes
Microwave setting: Maximum (Full)

30 g (1 oz) butter
1 cup cabbage, finely shredded
1 large potato, peeled and diced
1 medium onion, peeled and chopped
1 medium carrot, peeled and thinly sliced
1 cup cauliflower florets
½ turnip, peeled and diced
1×410 g can tomatoes with their juice
freshly ground black pepper
4 cups hot beef stock
salt

Place the butter, cabbage, potatoes, onions, carrots, cauliflower, turnip, tomatoes and pepper in a large bowl. Cover and cook for 10 minutes, stirring halfway through cooking.

Stir in the stock. Cover and cook for 10 minutes or until the vegetables are tender, stirring halfway through cooking.

Season with salt before serving.

TOMATO SOUP WITH RICE & BASIL

Serves 4-6 Cooking time: 18-19 minutes
Microwave setting: Maximum (Full)

30 g (1 oz) butter
1 large onion, peeled and chopped
2 tablespoons plain flour
2 tablespoons tomato paste
750 g (1½ lb) ripe tomatoes, cut into quarters
¼ teaspoon celery salt
1 teaspoon caster sugar
1 teaspoon chopped basil
freshly ground black pepper
1¼ cups milk
2 cups hot chicken stock
4 tablespoons cooked rice
salt
2 tablespoons cream, to serve (optional)

Place the butter and onion in a large bowl. Cover and cook for 4 minutes.

Stir in the flour and cook for 1 minute. Add tomato paste, tomatoes, celery salt, sugar, basil and pepper. Add the milk. Cover and cook for 10 minutes, stirring halfway through cooking.

Add the hot stock and allow to cool slightly.

Pour the soup into a blender and blend until smooth.

Sieve the liquidized soup to remove the tomato skins and pips. Stir in the cooked rice.

Return the soup to the bowl and reheat uncovered for 3-4 minutes. Season with salt.

Serve the soup with a swirl of cream floating on the top, if liked.

Country vegetable soup; Tomato soup with rice and basil

FISH SOUP

Serves 6 Cooking time: about 18 minutes
Microwave setting: Maximum (Full)

1 onion, peeled and finely chopped
1 small green pepper, seeded and finely diced
2 medium potatoes, peeled and finely diced
1 tablespoon oil
1 garlic clove, peeled and crushed
¼ teaspoon chopped rosemary
1 teaspoon chopped parsley
2 bay leaves
2½ cups cold water
750 g (1½ lb) filleted white fish, cut into small pieces
2 cups hot water
salt
freshly ground black pepper
lemon juice

Place the onion, green pepper, potatoes, oil, garlic, rosemary and parsley in a large bowl. Cover and cook for 8 minutes or until the vegetables are tender.

Stir in the bay leaves, cold water and fish. Cover and cook for 10 minutes, stirring halfway through.

Stir the hot water gently into the fish mixture.

Remove the bay leaves. Season with salt, pepper and lemon juice.

PEA & MINT SOUP

Serves 4 Cooking time: about 19 minutes
Microwave setting: Maximum (Full)

30 g (1 oz) butter
1 medium onion, peeled and finely chopped
500 g (1 lb) frozen peas
1 tablespoon chopped mint
2½ cups hot chicken stock
freshly ground black pepper
2 tablespoons cornflour
2 cups milk
salt
4 mint sprigs, to garnish

Place the butter, onion, peas and mint in a large bowl. Cover and cook for 8 minutes, stirring halfway through cooking.

Add the hot chicken stock and pepper. Cover and cook for 5 minutes.

Place the cornflour in a small bowl and gradually blend in the milk. Stir the milk into the soup.

Pour the soup into a blender in batches and blend until smooth.

Return the soup to the bowl, cover and cook for 6 minutes, stirring halfway through cooking.

Season with salt, then serve garnished with mint sprigs.

Fish soup; Pea and mint soup

LETTUCE SOUP WITH CROUTONS

Serves 4 Cooking time: about 14 minutes
Microwave setting: Maximum (Full)

1 medium onion, peeled and finely chopped
60 g (2 oz) butter
2 tablespoons plain flour
2 cups hot chicken stock
1¼ cups milk
250 g (8 oz) lettuce leaves, washed and chopped
¼ teaspoon grated nutmeg
¼ teaspoon caster sugar
freshly ground black pepper
1 egg yolk
salt
croutons (page 14), to serve

Place the onion and butter in a large bowl. Cover and cook for 2 minutes.

Stir in the flour and cook 1 minute. Add hot stock, milk, lettuce, nutmeg, sugar and pepper. Cover and cook for 9 minutes. Cool slightly.

Pour the soup and the egg yolk into a blender in batches and blend until smooth.

Return soup to the bowl. Reheat for 2 minutes.

Season with salt and serve garnished with croutons.

CHICKEN & VEGETABLE SOUP

Serves 4 Cooking time: about 26 minutes
Microwave setting: Maximum (Full)

1 carrot, peeled and finely sliced
1 medium potato, peeled and diced
4 button mushrooms, sliced
1 small red pepper, cored, seeded and diced
1 small turnip, peeled and diced
½ leek, trimmed and finely sliced
1 small onion, peeled and chopped
600 g (1¼ lb) chicken pieces, skinned
4 cups hot chicken stock
freshly ground black pepper
bouquet garni
2 teaspoons arrowroot
2 tablespoons sherry
salt

Place the carrot, potato, mushrooms, red pepper, turnip, leek and onion in a large bowl. Place the chicken pieces on top of the vegetables. Cover and cook for 15 minutes, stirring halfway through.

Add the hot chicken stock, pepper and bouquet garni. Cover and cook for 8 minutes.

Remove the bouquet garni. Take out the chicken and cut off the meat. Chop meat and return it to the soup.

Blend arrowroot and sherry. Stir into the soup and reheat for 3 minutes, stirring once. Season with salt.

Lettuce soup with croutons;
Chicken and vegetable soup

VICHYSSOISE

Serves 4-5 Cooking time: 14 minutes
Microwave setting: Maximum (Full)

375 g (12 oz) potatoes, peeled and thinly sliced
750 g (1½ lb) leeks, trimmed and thinly sliced
60 g (2 oz) butter
4 tablespoons water
3½ cups hot chicken stock
freshly ground black pepper
salt
¾ cup cream
1 tablespoon snipped chives, to garnish

Place the potatoes, leeks, butter and water in a large bowl. Cover and cook for 8 minutes, stirring halfway through cooking.

Add half the stock and a grinding of pepper. Cover and cook for 6 minutes. Add the remaining stock.

Pour the soup into a blender in batches and blend, then sieve and season with salt.

Allow to cool completely, then chill covered for 2 hours or longer.

Before serving, stir in the cream and check seasoning. Garnish with snipped chives.

MUSHROOM SOUP

Serves 4 Cooking time: about 13½ minutes
Microwave setting: Maximum (Full)

30 g (1 oz) butter
1 medium onion, peeled and finely chopped
250 g (8 oz) flat mushrooms, chopped
2 tablespoons plain flour
1¼ cups milk
freshly ground black pepper
2½ cups hot chicken stock
4 tablespoons cream
salt
2 button mushrooms, thinly sliced, to garnish

Place the butter and onion in a large bowl, cover and cook for 2 minutes. Stir in the chopped mushrooms, cover and cook for 3 minutes.

Stir in the flour, cook for 2 minutes, then gradually blend in the milk and season with pepper. Cover and cook for 3½ minutes.

Stir in the hot stock. Puree in batches in a blender, then pour back into the bowl.

Stir in the cream and season with salt. Reheat uncovered for 3 minutes if required.

Pour into 4 soup bowls and garnish with the sliced mushrooms.

Vichyssoise; Mushroom soup

Artichokes with French dressing;
Mushrooms in garlic butter

STARTERS

ARTICHOKES WITH FRENCH DRESSING

Serves 4 Cooking time: 9-12 minutes, plus standing
Microwave setting: Maximum (Full)

4 artichokes
2 cups water
2 tablespoons lemon juice

Dressing:
½ teaspoon salt
freshly ground black pepper
1 teaspoon Dijon mustard
4 tablespoons wine vinegar
¾ cup olive oil

With kitchen scissors, trim off points from outer leaves of artichokes. Trim off stalks. Rinse artichokes in water with 1 tablespoon lemon juice added and turn upside down to drain.

Sprinkle the artichokes with remaining lemon juice and wrap each one in plastic film.

Arrange the artichokes round a plate and cook for 9-12 minutes, until bases are tender when pricked with a fork. Turn each artichoke round halfway through cooking.

Leave to stand, wrapped, for 2-4 minutes then unwrap and leave to cool.

To make the dressing, mix the salt, pepper, mustard and vinegar in a small bowl. Whisk in the oil a little at a time until thick.

To serve, spoon a little dressing over each artichoke. Hand the remaining dressing separately.

MUSHROOMS IN GARLIC BUTTER

Serves 4 Cooking time: about 6½ minutes
Microwave setting: Maximum (Full)

500 g (1 lb) button mushrooms
2 garlic cloves, peeled and crushed
1 tablespoon lemon juice
125 g (4 oz) butter, cut into pieces
1 tablespoon cream
2 tablespoons chopped parsley
freshly ground black pepper
salt

Place the mushrooms, garlic and lemon juice in a large bowl. Cover and cook for 4 minutes. Pour off any excess liquid.

Stir in the butter, cream, parsley and pepper. Cook, uncovered, for 2½ minutes, stirring every minute. Season with salt and serve with crusty bread.

HOT CRAB

Serves 4 Cooking time: 3 minutes
Microwave setting: Maximum (Full)

1 cup fresh white breadcrumbs
2 teaspoons oil
2 teaspoons anchovy sauce
1 tablespoon lemon juice
1 tablespoon Worcestershire sauce
½ cup cream
185 g (6 oz) crab meat
freshly ground black pepper
salt
4 pieces fried bread (page 15)

To garnish:
paprika
parsley sprigs

Place the breadcrumbs, oil, anchovy sauce, lemon juice, Worcestershire sauce, cream, crab meat and black pepper in a bowl and mix them all together thoroughly.

Cook for 3 minutes, stirring every minute. Season with salt.

Spoon on to the fried bread and serve garnished with paprika and a sprig of parsley.

Note: Frozen crab meat, thawed and drained, may be used.

ROLLMOPS

Serves 4 Cooking time: about 9 minutes
Microwave setting: Maximum (Full)

8 fillets of mullet, herring or large garfish
1 large onion, peeled and finely sliced
1¼ cups cider vinegar
1 teaspoon caster sugar
salt
freshly ground black pepper
1 teaspoon mixed spice
2 teaspoons pickling spice
4 bay leaves

Roll up each fish fillet with the skin to the outside and place in a shallow dish. Scatter the onion over the top of the fish.

Mix together the remaining ingredients. Pour over the fish and onion. Cover and cook for 5 minutes. Turn the plate round and cook for a further 4 minutes. Leave to cool before serving. Garnish with a couple of the bay leaves.

COQUILLES ST JACQUES

Serves 4 Cooking time: 15 minutes
Microwave setting: Maximum (Full)

500 g (1 lb) potatoes, peeled and roughly diced into 2.5 cm (1 inch) cubes
3 tablespoons water
salt
125 g (4 oz) button mushrooms, sliced
1 garlic clove, peeled and crushed
60 g (2 oz) butter
1½ tablespoons cornflour
½ cup dry white wine
1 egg yolk
375 g (12 oz) scallops, sliced if large
2 tablespoons cream
freshly ground black pepper
1 tablespoon milk

To garnish:
4 parsley sprigs
1 scallop, sliced

Place the potatoes in a medium bowl with the water and a pinch of salt. Cover and cook for 8 minutes, stirring halfway through cooking. Leave to stand, covered, while making the sauce.

Place the mushrooms, garlic and 30 g (1 oz) of the butter in a medium bowl. Cover, cook for 3 minutes. Mix the cornflour and wine and stir in. Cook uncovered for 2 minutes.

Beat in the egg yolk, then stir in the scallops, cream and salt and pepper to taste. Cook uncovered for 2 minutes.

Meanwhile, mash the potatoes with the remaining butter, the milk and salt and pepper to taste. Place in a piping bag fitted with a large star nozzle and pipe around the edges of 4 scallop shells.

Spoon the sauce into the centre. Reheat if necessary. Serve garnished with parsley and scallop.

HOT SEAFOOD COCKTAIL

Serves 4 Cooking time: 9½ minutes
Microwave setting: Maximum (Full)

60 g (2 oz) butter
4 tablespoons plain flour
2½ cups milk
freshly ground black pepper
salt
2 teaspoons tomato paste
90 g (3 oz) scallops
90 g (3 oz) cooked mussels
90 g (3 oz) cooked, peeled prawns

To garnish:
mild paprika
whole cooked prawns
4 lemon slices

Place the butter in a bowl and cook for 1½ minutes.

Stir in the flour and cook 1 minute, then gradually blend in the milk and pepper. Cook for 4 minutes, stirring every minute. Season with salt.

Add the tomato paste. Stir in the scallops, mussels and prawns. Cook for 3 minutes, stirring halfway through cooking.

Place the mixture in a large dish. Garnish with a sprinkling of paprika, whole prawns and lemon slices. Serve immediately.

Clockwise:
Coquilles St Jacques; Hot seafood cocktail; Rollmops; Hot crab

RATATOUILLE

Serves 4-6 Cooking time: 15-20 minutes
Microwave setting: Maximum (Full)

2 zucchini, sliced
1 medium eggplant, sliced
6 tomatoes, skinned and chopped
½ green pepper, seeded and finely sliced
½ red pepper, seeded and finely sliced
1 medium onion, peeled and sliced
1 tablespoon tomato paste
2 garlic cloves, peeled and crushed
6 tablespoons olive oil
freshly ground black pepper
salt

Place the zucchini, eggplant, tomatoes, green and red peppers, onion, tomato paste, garlic, oil and pepper in a large bowl.

Cover and cook for 15-20 minutes, stirring several times during cooking.

Season with salt, then allow to cool. Serve with crusty bread.

HONEYED GRAPEFRUIT & ORANGE

Serves 4 Cooking time: 3½ minutes
Microwave setting: Maximum (Full)

2 large grapefruit, halved, segmented, drained, with shells reserved
1 large orange, pith and skin removed, segmented and drained
1 tablespoon honey
1 tablespoon brown sugar

Place the grapefruit and orange segments in a bowl. Add the honey. Cook for 1½ minutes.

Divide the mixture between the grapefruit shells. Sprinkle the sugar over each.

Stand the halves on a plate or in individual dishes. Cook for 2 minutes.

From left to right: Ratatouille; Honeyed grapefruit and orange; Jellied ham and chicken; Corn-on-the-cob with parsley butter

JELLIED HAM & CHICKEN

Serves 4 Cooking time: about 2½ minutes, plus setting
Microwave setting: Maximum (Full)

125 g (4 oz) cooked chicken meat, finely diced
125 g (4 oz) cooked ham, finely chopped
3 teaspoons gelatine
1¾ cups well-flavoured chicken stock
1 tablespoon vermouth
2 teaspoons chopped parsley
salt
freshly ground black pepper
4 cucumber slices, to garnish

Mix together the chicken and ham and divide among 4 pots.

Place the gelatine in a bowl and slowly stir in half the stock. Cook for 2½ minutes or until the gelatine has dissolved, stirring after each minute.

Stir in the vermouth, parsley and remaining stock. Season with salt and pepper. Cool, then pour over the chicken and ham. Chill until set.

Garnish each pot with cucumber.

CORN-ON-THE-COB WITH PARSLEY BUTTER

Serves 4 Cooking time: about 14 minutes
Microwave setting: Maximum (Full)

90 g (3 oz) butter
4 cobs corn, fresh or frozen
2 tablespoons finely chopped parsley
black pepper

Cut the butter into pieces and place in a small dish. Heat for 1½ minutes or until melted.

Brush the corn with melted butter and wrap each cob in greaseproof paper.

Arrange the corn in a shallow container. Cover and cook for 10 minutes if fresh, or 12 minutes if frozen, until the corn is tender when pricked with a fork or skewer.

Remove the corn from the greaseproof paper and put into individual dishes.

Stir the parsley into the remaining butter, add a grinding of pepper and reheat for 45 seconds. Pour the hot parsley butter over the corn.

PRAWNS IN BRANDY SAUCE

Serves 4 Cooking time: 12 minutes
Microwave setting: Maximum (Full)

2 garlic cloves, peeled and crushed
1 medium onion, peeled and finely chopped
30 g (1 oz) butter
1½ tablespoons cornflour
1¼ cups milk
2 teaspoons tomato paste
2 tablespoons brandy
1 tablespoon cream
500 g (1 lb) shelled green prawns
freshly ground black pepper
salt

To garnish:
chopped parsley
lemon wedges

Place the garlic, onion and butter in a large bowl. Cover and cook for 4 minutes.

Stir in the cornflour, then blend in the milk, tomato paste, brandy, cream, prawns and pepper. Cook uncovered for 8 minutes, stirring halfway through. Season with salt.

Sprinkle with parsley and serve with lemon.

PRAWNS WITH GARLIC & TOMATOES

Serves 2 Cooking time: 7 minutes
Microwave setting: Maximum (Full)

30 g (1 oz) butter
½ onion, peeled and grated
250 g (8 oz) small cooked, shelled prawns
4 tomatoes, skinned and finely chopped
2 garlic cloves, peeled and crushed
1 tablespoon tomato paste
½ teaspoon ground mace
freshly ground black pepper
salt

Place the butter and onion in a large bowl, cover and cook for 2 minutes.

Stir in the prawns, tomatoes, garlic, tomato paste, mace and pepper. Cover and cook for 5 minutes, stirring halfway through.

Season with salt before serving.

Prawns with garlic and tomatoes;
Prawns in brandy sauce

PRAWN & LEMON PANCAKES

Serves 4 Cooking time: 8¾ minutes, plus pancakes
Microwave setting: Maximum (Full)

1 small egg
1 egg yolk
1¼ cups milk
pinch of salt
1 cup plain flour
oil, for frying

Filling:
45 g (1½ oz) butter
2½ tablespoons plain flour
1¼ cups milk
freshly ground black pepper
1 teaspoon anchovy sauce
salt
grated rind of 1 small lemon
185 g (6 oz) cooked, shelled prawns

Beat together the egg, egg yolk and milk. Place the salt and flour in a mixing bowl, make a well in the centre and pour in the egg mixture. Stir, gradually incorporating the flour into the liquid, and stand, covered, for 30 minutes.

Make 8 pancakes using the conventional stove top. Keep warm while making the filling.

Place the butter in a bowl. Cook for 45 seconds or until melted.

Stir in the flour and cook 1 minute. Gradually blend in the milk and pepper to taste. Cook for 4 minutes, stirring every minute.

Add the anchovy sauce and season with salt. Stir in the lemon rind and prawns.

Spread the mixture in a line down the centre of each pancake and fold edges over.

Divide the pancakes between 2 plates. Cook each plate of pancakes for 1½ minutes.

TOMATO PASTA BOWS

Serves 4 Cooking time: 13 minutes, plus standing
Microwave setting: Maximum (Full)

8 cups boiling water
1 tablespoon oil
salt
250 g (8 oz) pasta bows

Sauce:
1 medium onion, peeled and finely chopped
2 garlic cloves, peeled and crushed
1 teaspoon cornflour
1×410 g can tomatoes, chopped with their juice
2 teaspoons chopped oregano
2 tablespoons tomato paste
freshly ground black pepper
salt
15 g (½ oz) butter
2 tablespoons grated Parmesan cheese

Place the boiling water, oil, salt and pasta in a large bowl. Cover and cook for 8 minutes. Leave to stand, covered, for 10 minutes.

Place the onion and garlic in a small bowl, cover and cook for 2 minutes. Stir in the cornflour, tomatoes, oregano, tomato paste and pepper. Cook uncovered 3 minutes, stirring halfway through. Season with salt.

Drain the pasta and stir in the sauce and butter. Serve sprinkled with Parmesan cheese.

Prawn and lemon pancakes;
Tomato pasta bows

LIVER PATE

Serves 4 Cooking time: about 7½ minutes
Microwave setting: Maximum (Full)

2 bacon rashers, rinds removed and chopped
250 g (8 oz) chicken livers
1 garlic clove, peeled and crushed
155 g (5 oz) butter
½ teaspoon freshly grated nutmeg
freshly ground black pepper
1 tablespoon dry sherry
1 tablespoon cream

Place the bacon in a medium bowl. Cook for 2 minutes. Trim livers of fibres.

Add the livers, garlic, 125 g (4 oz) of the butter, nutmeg and pepper. Cover and cook for 5 minutes, stirring halfway through cooking.

Add the sherry and cream. Place the mixture in a food processor and process until smooth. Spoon into 4 ramekin dishes or 1 large dish.

Place the remaining butter in a bowl. Cook for 30 seconds or until melted. Pour a little butter over each serving of the pate.

Allow to cool completely, then chill for 2 hours.

KIPPER PATE

Serves 4 Cooking time: 6 minutes
Microwave setting: Maximum (Full)

250 g (8 oz) kipper fillets
1 small onion, peeled and chopped
60 g (2 oz) butter
90 g (3 oz) cream cheese
¼ teaspoon ground mace
1 tablespoon lemon juice
salt
freshly ground black pepper
parsley sprigs, to garnish

Place the kippers in a shallow dish. Cover and cook for 4 minutes, turning once. Set aside.

Place the onion and butter in a bowl, cover and cook for 2 minutes.

Chop the kippers and add to the onion and butter. Stir in the cream cheese, mace, lemon juice, salt and pepper. Place the mixture in a food processor and process until smooth.

Divide the pate among 4 ramekin dishes. Allow to cool completely then chill for 2 hours. Garnish with parsley sprigs.

Liver pate; Kipper pate

STUFFED TOMATOES

Serves 4 Cooking time: about 5½ minutes
Microwave setting: Maximum (Full)

4 large tomatoes, about 750 g (1½ lb)
¾ cup fresh brown breadcrumbs
2 tablespoons finely grated Cheddar cheese
30 g (1 oz) chopped ham
2 teaspoons chopped, mixed herbs
1 teaspoon made English mustard
2 tablespoons plain yogurt
salt
freshly ground black pepper
4 parsley sprigs, to garnish

Cut out blossom marks from the tomatoes, slice off the tops and reserve. Using a grapefruit knife, scoop out the centres. Chop the flesh, then mix with the remaining ingredients except parsley.

Fill tomatoes with the stuffing and replace the tops.

Place the tomatoes in 4 small dishes and arrange in a circle in the oven. Cook uncovered for 5½ minutes or until soft, rearranging halfway through cooking. Remove any which may be cooked before the total cooking time.

Garnish each tomato with a sprig of parsley.

STUFFED BAKED AVOCADO WITH PRAWNS

Serves 4 Cooking time: about 5 minutes
Microwave setting: Maximum (Full)

30 g (1 oz) butter
1 cup fresh brown breadcrumbs
1 tablespoon grated lemon rind
125 g (4 oz) cooked, shelled prawns
5 tablespoons cream
salt
freshly ground black pepper
2 large ripe avocados
1 tablespoon lemon juice

To garnish:
lettuce leaves
lemon twists

Place the butter in a bowl. Cook for 30 seconds or until melted.

Stir in the breadcrumbs. Cook for 1 minute. Stir in lemon rind, prawns, cream, salt and pepper.

Cut the avocados in half. Remove and discard the stones, then brush the flesh with lemon juice.

Pile the prawn mixture into each of the avocado halves. Arrange on a plate. Cook for 3½ minutes.

Serve on lettuce, garnished with lemon.

Stuffed tomatoes; Stuffed baked avocado with prawns

EGGS, CHEESE & CREAM

CURRIED EGGS

Serves 4 Cooking time: 9 minutes, plus boiling eggs
Microwave setting: Maximum (Full)

4 eggs
1 medium onion, peeled and finely chopped
1 garlic clove, peeled and crushed
1 tablespoon tomato paste
1 tablespoon lemon juice
1 tablespoon curry powder
1 teaspoon Mexican-style chilli powder
2 tablespoons white wine vinegar
15 g (½ oz) butter
1 tablespoon flour
1¼ cups hot chicken stock
4 lemon slices, to garnish

Place the eggs in a saucepan and cover with water. Bring to the boil and **cook the eggs conventionally on the stove-top** for 8 minutes to hard-boil.

Meanwhile, place the onion, garlic, tomato paste, lemon juice, curry powder, chilli powder and vinegar in a medium bowl. Cover and cook for 5 minutes, stirring halfway through cooking.

Stir in the butter until melted. Stir in the flour and cook 1 minute. Blend in the stock and cook uncovered for 3 minutes, stirring every minute.

Plunge the eggs into cold water and remove the shells. Cut each egg in half and arrange, cut sides down, on a serving dish. Strain the sauce and pour over eggs. Garnish with lemon slices.

Serve with boiled rice, sliced tomatoes and desiccated coconut.

Curried eggs

FRIED EGGS

Serves 2 Cooking time: about 1¾ minutes, plus standing
Microwave setting: Maximum (Full)

1 tablespoon butter
2 eggs, taken from refrigerator
freshly ground black pepper (optional)

Divide the butter between two 13 cm (5 inch) top diameter shallow dishes or saucers. Cook for 30 seconds or until melted.

Break an egg into each dish and pierce the yolk with a cocktail stick. Sprinkle with pepper, if desired. Cover tightly with plastic film.

Cook for 1¼ minutes, turning round halfway through cooking. Leave to stand, covered, for 1 minute before serving. If the egg is not cooked, return to the oven for 15 seconds.

From left to right: Fried eggs; Baked eggs; Omelette; Poached eggs

BAKED EGGS

Serves 4 Cooking time: 4½ minutes
Microwave setting: Maximum (Full)

1 tablespoon butter
2 small mushrooms, finely chopped
60 g (2 oz) ham, finely chopped
4 small eggs
salt
freshly ground black pepper
4 tablespoons cream

Divide the butter and mushrooms among 4 ramekins or small individual souffle dishes. Cook for 1½ minutes.

Place the ham on the mushrooms.

Break the eggs on to the ham and pierce the yolks with a cocktail stick. Season with salt and pepper.

Pour 1 tablespoon cream over each of the eggs. Cover and cook for 1½ minutes.

Rearrange the dishes, so the front ones are at the back, and cook for a further 1½ minutes. Serve the eggs at once.

OMELETTE

Serves 2 Cooking time: 3¾ minutes
Microwave setting: Maximum (Full)

4 eggs
4 tablespoons water
salt
freshly ground black pepper
1 tablespoon butter
1 tablespoon chopped parsley or fresh herbs, to garnish

Place the eggs, water and salt and pepper in a bowl, beat with a fork.

Place the butter in a 23 cm (9 inch) tart plate. Cook, uncovered, for 30 seconds.

Tilt the plate to be sure the bottom is evenly coated with melted butter, then pour in the egg mixture. Cover and cook for 2 minutes.

Using a fork, draw the edges of the egg to the centre. Cover and cook for a further 1¼ minutes. If not quite cooked, stand for 1 minute before serving.

Serve sprinkled with chopped parsley or herbs.

Variation:
Chopped ham could be added after the cooking is completed.

POACHED EGGS

Serves 2 Cooking time: about 3 minutes, plus standing
Microwave setting: Maximum (Full)

½ cup water
½ teaspoon white vinegar
2 eggs
hot buttered toast, to serve

Divide the water and vinegar equally between 2 ramekins. Cook uncovered for 2 minutes or until boiling.

Break the eggs into the water and cook covered for 1 minute.

Leave the eggs to stand for 1 minute.

Drain off the water and vinegar, then serve on hot buttered toast.

BOILED EGGS

Eggs in shells cannot be cooked in a microwave oven unless great care is taken, and I do not advise attempting this. If eggs should burst it not only makes a mess of the oven but can actually damage it, so this is one time when it is best to stick to the conventional cooking method.

EGGS BENEDICT

Serves 4 Cooking time: about 4½ minutes
Microwave setting: Maximum (Full)

4 slices of cooked ham
4 thick slices of buttered white toast, cut to the size of the ham

Poached eggs:
1 cup water
2 teaspoons white vinegar
4 eggs

Hollandaise sauce:
2 egg yolks
1 tablespoon lemon juice
125 g (4 oz) butter, cut into 8 pieces
pinch of cayenne pepper

Place a piece of ham on each slice of toast and keep warm.

Divide the water and vinegar equally among 4 ramekins. Cook uncovered for 2 minutes or until boiling. Break an egg into each dish.

To make the sauce, prick the egg yolks and place with the lemon juice in a small bowl. Cook uncovered for 30 seconds. Beat hard until smooth.

Place the eggs for poaching into the oven and cook covered for 2 minutes. Stand for 1 minute before draining.

Meanwhile, beat a piece of butter at a time into the sauce, until all 8 pieces are incorporated. Beat in the cayenne pepper.

Place the poached eggs on the ham and toast and top with a large spoonful of sauce. Serve at once.

EGGS FLORENTINE

Serves 4 Cooking time: 3¾-4½ minutes
Microwave setting: Maximum (Full)

250 g (8 oz) frozen spinach, thawed and drained
salt
freshly ground black pepper
¼ teaspoon grated nutmeg
4 eggs, from refrigerator

Divide the spinach among 4 ramekins. Cook uncovered for 1½ minutes.

Sprinkle the spinach with salt, pepper and nutmeg. Break the eggs on to the spinach. Prick the yolks and cover dishes with plastic film. Arrange in a circle in the oven.

Cook for 2¼-3 minutes, rearranging the dishes halfway through cooking. If the eggs are not quite cooked, allow to stand, covered, for 1 minute.

Serve with hot buttered toast.

Eggs Benedict; Eggs Florentine

WELSH RAREBIT

Serves 4 Cooking time: 1½ minutes, plus grilling
Microwave setting: Maximum (Full)

2 cups finely grated Cheddar cheese
2 tablespoons milk
2 tablespoons beer (can be flat)
salt
freshly ground black pepper
1 teaspoon French mustard
4 slices toast
paprika (optional)
parsley sprigs, to garnish

Place the cheese, milk and beer in a medium bowl and cook for 1 minute. Stir in the salt, pepper and mustard and cook for 30 seconds.

Spread the cheese mixture over the slices of toast, sprinkle with paprika if using and garnish with the parsley sprigs.

If desired, omit paprika, which is used to add colour, and **brown the rarebit under a preheated conventional grill.**

CHEESE & HAM PUDDING

Serves 4 Cooking time: 10-12 minutes
Microwave setting: Maximum (Full)

4 cups fresh brown breadcrumbs
60 g (2 oz) cooked ham, finely chopped
pinch of dry mustard
1 tablespoon finely snipped chives
1½ cups finely grated mild Cheddar cheese
3 eggs, lightly beaten
2½ cups milk
salt
freshly ground black pepper
1 tablespoon chopped parsley, to garnish

Mix together the breadcrumbs, ham, mustard, chives and cheese. Lightly beat the eggs and milk into the mixture and season with salt and pepper. Pour into a souffle dish or ring mould. Allow to stand for 10 minutes.

Cook uncovered for 10-12 minutes, stirring halfway through cooking.

Sprinkle with parsley and serve with a green vegetable.

Welsh rarebit; Cheese and ham pudding

SALAMI & CHEESE TART

Serves 4-5 Cooking time: 8½ minutes, plus grilling
Microwave setting: Maximum (Full)

185 g (6 oz) prepared shortcrust pastry
½ cup milk
3 eggs
90 g (3 oz) salami, finely diced
salt
freshly ground black pepper
½ cup grated Samsoe or Cheddar cheese
parsley sprig, to garnish

The results of this tart may not be quite the same as if cooked by the conventional method. However, the flavour is excellent and it is a speedy dish to make. The egg mixture will still be wet in the centre after microwave cooking, but it sets during grilling.

Roll out the pastry and line a 20 cm (8 inch) pie plate. Prick the sides and base with a fork. Cook for 3½ minutes or until the pastry looks dry. Set aside.

Place the milk, eggs, salami, salt and pepper in a bowl. Lightly beat together. Cook for 2 minutes, beating with a fork every ½ minute.

Pour the mixture into the pastry case and cook for 3 minutes, stirring every minute.

Sprinkle the cheese over the egg and **brown under a preheated conventional grill** for about 5 minutes.

Garnish with the parsley.

SMOKED HADDOCK WITH EGG SAUCE

Serves 4 Cooking time: 15-16 minutes
Microwave setting: Maximum (Full)

1¼ cups milk
1 bay leaf
1 onion slice
750 g (1½ lb) smoked haddock
60 g (2 oz) butter
2 tablespoons plain flour
salt
freshly ground black pepper
2 hard-boiled eggs, finely chopped
2 tablespoons snipped chives

Place the milk in a jug with the bay leaf and onion slice and cook for 2 minutes. Leave for 15 minutes.

Place the haddock in a shallow dish and dot with half the butter. Cover and cook for 6-7 minutes, turning the dish round halfway through. Keep warm.

Place the remaining butter in a bowl. Cook for 1 minute or until melted. Blend in the flour and cook for 1 minute.

Strain the hot milk, discarding the bay leaf and onion, and stir in. Add salt and pepper. Cook for 3 minutes, stirring every minute.

Stir in the chopped hard-boiled eggs and chives.

Pour the sauce over the fish and reheat for 2 minutes before serving.

Salami and cheese tart; Smoked haddock with egg sauce

BREAKFAST FOR TWO

2 slices of toast, halved (optional)
Kidneys, mushrooms and bacon
Scrambled eggs

Order of cooking:

Toast the bread in the conventional manner. Cook the kidneys, mushrooms and bacon as directed. Cover and keep hot.

Make the scrambled eggs.

Warm the toast (if using) for 30 seconds on a piece of paper towel, and serve.

SCRAMBLED EGGS

Serves 2 Cooking time: 3-5 minutes, plus toasting
Microwave setting: Maximum (Full) or Medium (½ power)

4 eggs
1 tablespoon milk
salt
freshly ground black pepper
15 g (½ oz) butter
hot buttered toast, to serve
2 parsley sprigs, to garnish (optional)

Place the eggs, milk, salt and pepper to taste in a large bowl and beat well. Add the butter.

Cook uncovered for about 3 minutes on Maximum or 5 minutes on Medium (for a creamier result). Break up the mixture and beat gently after every minute.

Serve on hot buttered toast garnished with parsley (if using).

KIDNEYS, MUSHROOMS & BACON

Serves 2 Cooking time: 5½ minutes
Microwave setting: Maximum (Full)

4 rashers streaky bacon, rinds removed
4 flat mushrooms
2 lamb's kidneys, membrane and core removed and halved

Place a piece of paper towel on a plate. Place the bacon on one side, cover with another piece of paper and cook for 1 minute.

Uncover. Place the mushrooms in the centre of the plate, cover and cook for 1½ minutes, then put the kidneys round the outside of the plate, re-cover, and cook for 2 minutes, turning the kidneys over and rearranging the mushrooms if necessary. Re-cover and cook for 1 minute.

Serve at once. Or, if being served with scrambled egg, remove the paper towels and cover with a plate to keep hot while cooking the eggs.

Scrambled eggs; Kidneys, mushrooms and bacon

Tournedos Provencals

BEEF

TOURNEDOS PROVENCALS

Serves 4 Cooking time: 14-16 minutes
Microwave setting: Maximum (Full)

1 medium onion, peeled and chopped
60 g (2 oz) button mushrooms, peeled and sliced
1 garlic clove, peeled and crushed
1 teaspoon chopped thyme
1 teaspoon chopped oregano
¼ teaspoon chopped rosemary
30 g (1 oz) butter, cut into pieces
1½ tablespoons plain flour
2 tablespoons tomato paste
1¼ cups hot beef stock
freshly ground black pepper
salt
4 fillet steaks, 2.5 cm (1 inch) thick, 8-10 cm (3-4 inches) wide, total weight 600 g (1¼ lb)
15 g (½ oz) butter, melted
4 slices fried bread, 5 mm (¼ inch) thick (page 15)

Place the onion, mushrooms, garlic, thyme, oregano and rosemary in a bowl. Cover and cook for 3 minutes.

Stir in the butter until melted. Stir in the flour and cook 1 minute. Blend in the tomato paste, stock and pepper. Cook uncovered for 4 minutes, stirring every minute. Season with salt and set aside, covered.

Brush steaks with melted butter and place on a preheated browning dish. Cook uncovered for 3-5 minutes, depending on how rare you like your steak, and turning over and rearranging halfway through. Pour the steak juices into the sauce.

Cut the fried bread to fit the steaks. Place steak on top. Cook uncovered for 3 minutes.

Spoon over the sauce and serve with a green salad.

GARLIC ROAST BEEF

Serves 6-8 Cooking time: 17 minutes, plus standing
Microwave setting: Maximum (Full)

1.5 kg (3 lb) yearling topside or rump
oil, to coat
3 garlic cloves, peeled
freshly ground black pepper

Tie the beef into a compact shape and rub with the oil, 1 garlic clove and pepper.

Place the beef on a preheated browning dish, fat side down if rump, cover with a paper towel and cook for 10 minutes, turning once.

With a sharp knife, cut the remaining garlic cloves into slivers. Make incisions in the meat and insert the slivers of garlic.

Cook for 7 minutes, turning once.

Remove the meat and tent loosely with foil, with the shiny side inside. Leave the meat to stand for 20 minutes, then carve.

BEEF OLIVES

Serves 4 Cooking time: 13 minutes
Microwave setting: Maximum (Full)

60 g (2 oz) mushrooms
1 onion, peeled and quartered
1 tablespoon orange juice
3 tablespoons beef stock
grated rind of 1 lemon
1 teaspoon chopped, mixed herbs
salt
freshly ground black pepper
½ cup fresh white breadcrumbs
500 g (1 lb) yearling topside, cut into 4 thin slices and lightly beaten
½ green pepper, cored, seeded and chopped
125 g (4 oz) mushrooms, chopped
45 g (1½ oz) butter, diced
1 tablespoon plain flour
½ cup white wine
1 teaspoon soy sauce
chopped parsley, to garnish

Puree the whole mushrooms, onion, orange juice, stock, lemon rind, herbs and salt and pepper in a food processor. Stir in the breadcrumbs.

Divide mixture among the beef slices, roll up and tie. Cook uncovered 6 minutes, turning over halfway. Remove string. Set aside, covered.

Cook the green pepper and mushrooms, covered, in a large bowl for 2 minutes. Stir in the butter until melted. Stir in the flour, cook 1 minute, add wine, soy sauce and meat juices. Season. Pour over the beef. Cook for 4 minutes. Garnish with parsley.

Garlic roast beef; Beef olives

TARRAGON BEEF

Serves 4 Cooking time: 10 minutes
Microwave setting: Maximum (Full)

3 tablespoons chopped fresh tarragon
4 fillet steaks, total weight 750 g (1½ lb), lightly beaten
30 g (1 oz) butter, melted
½ cup beef stock
1 tablespoon cornflour
2 tablespoons water
salt
freshly ground black pepper
6 tablespoons cream
fresh tarragon, to garnish

Sprinkle 2 tablespoons of the tarragon over both sides of the steaks and rub in well. Brush the steaks with half the butter, place on a preheated browning dish and cook, uncovered for 7 minutes, turning over and rearranging halfway through cooking.

Remove steaks and keep warm. Add stock to browning dish and stir, scraping up brown bits.

Place the remaining butter in a large bowl and add the stock and meat juices from the browning dish. Blend the cornflour and water and stir in with the remaining tarragon and salt and pepper to taste. Cook uncovered for 3 minutes, stirring every minute.

Stir in the cream and pour over the steaks. Reheat for 1 minute if necessary. Garnish with tarragon and serve with a green salad.

Tarragon beef

BEEF IN BEER

Serves 4 Cooking time: 53 minutes, plus standing
Microwave setting: Maximum (Full) and Defrost

1 medium onion, peeled and sliced
2 small carrots, peeled and sliced
1 celery stick, chopped
600 g (1¼ lb) topside beef, cut into cubes
30 g (1 oz) butter, diced
2 tablespoons plain flour
1 tablespoon tomato paste
2 teaspoons chopped, mixed herbs
½ cup beer
1¼ cups hot beef stock
freshly ground black pepper
salt

Place the onion, carrots and celery in a large bowl. Cover and cook on Maximum for 5 minutes, stirring halfway through cooking.

Stir in the beef, butter and flour, cover and cook on Maximum for 3 minutes. Stir in remaining ingredients except salt. Cover and cook 5 minutes.

Cook uncovered for a further 40 minutes on Defrost, stirring several times. Add salt toward end of cooking.

Stand, covered, for 10 minutes before serving. Serve with boiled noodles.

BEEF IN CIDER

Serves 6 Cooking time: 52 minutes, plus standing
Microwave setting: Maximum (Full) and Defrost

½ green pepper, cored, seeded and finely chopped
2 medium onions, peeled and thinly sliced
1 kg (2 lb) silverside beef, trimmed and cubed
45 g (1½ oz) butter, cut into pieces
2½ tablespoons plain flour
1 bay leaf
1 teaspoon chopped oregano
1 teaspoon chopped thyme
1 tablespoon tomato paste
1¼ cups dry cider
½ cup hot beef stock
freshly ground black pepper
salt

Place the green pepper and onions in a large bowl, cover and cook on Maximum for 5 minutes.

Stir in the beef, butter and flour. Cover and cook on Maximum for 7 minutes, stirring twice.

Stir in the remaining ingredients except salt. Cover and cook on Defrost for 40 minutes, stirring twice and adding salt toward end of cooking. Leave to stand, covered, for 10 minutes.

Discard the bay leaf before serving.

BEEF GOULASH

Serves 4 Cooking time: 50 minutes, plus standing
Microwave setting: Medium (½ power)

600 g (1¼ lb) beef topside, cubed
1 tablespoon paprika
1 large onion, peeled and sliced
1 large potato, peeled and sliced
2 tablespoons tomato paste
2 teaspoons caster sugar
2 tomatoes, skinned and chopped
1 cup hot beef stock
freshly ground black pepper
salt
2 tablespoons sour cream
paprika, to garnish

Place the meat in a shallow casserole. Combine the remaining ingredients except the salt, sour cream and extra paprika, and pour over the meat.

Cover tightly and cook on Medium for 25 minutes.

Stir thoroughly, breaking up potato. Cover again and cook for a further 25 minutes or until meat is tender, add salt toward the end of cooking. Stand for 10 minutes, covered.

Stir in the sour cream and sprinkle with paprika. Serve with ribbon noodles.

BEEF STROGANOFF

Serves 4-6 Cooking time: 10 minutes
Microwave setting: Maximum (Full)

60 g (2 oz) butter
750 g (1½ lb) beef fillet, cut into strips, 8×1 cm (3 inches×½ inch)
2 tablespoons plain flour
1 tablespoon tomato paste
1 large onion, peeled and finely diced
185 g (6 oz) mushrooms, sliced
½ cup dry white wine
freshly ground black pepper
salt
¼ cup sour cream
chopped parsley, to garnish

Heat the butter in a shallow casserole until bubbling. Toss the beef strips in the flour, add to casserole and cook, uncovered, for 5 minutes.

Stir in the remaining ingredients except the salt, sour cream and parsley. Cover and cook for 5 minutes, stirring halfway through cooking.

Stir in the sour cream, add salt to taste and serve, garnished with parsley, on a bed of boiled rice.

Left: Beef in beer; Beef in cider.
Right: Beef goulash; Beef stroganoff

BEEF, MUSHROOM & ONION SUET PUDDING

Serves 4 Cooking time: 17 minutes
Microwave setting: Maximum (Full)

Pastry:
2 cups self-raising flour
½ teaspoon salt
125 g (4 oz) shredded suet
about ¾ cup water

Filling:
30 g (1 oz) butter
2 medium onions, peeled and sliced
125 g (4 oz) mushrooms, chopped
1 garlic clove, peeled and crushed
1 teaspoon chopped parsley
¼ teaspoon chopped rosemary
½ teaspoon chopped oregano
½ teaspoon chopped marjoram
375 g (12 oz) minced beef
1 tablespoon flour
1 teaspoon Parisian essence
salt
freshly ground black pepper
parsley sprig, to garnish

Mix together the flour, salt, suet and enough water to form a smooth dough. Roll out ⅔ of the pastry and use to line a greased 5-cup pudding basin. Roll out the remainder for a lid and set aside.

Place the butter, onions, mushrooms, garlic and herbs in a medium bowl. Cover and cook for 4 minutes.

Stir in the beef, flour and Parisian essence. Cook uncovered for 4 minutes, stirring halfway through cooking. Season with salt and pepper.

Fill the basin with the mixture. Place the pastry lid in position and seal. Cover the dish loosely with plastic film and cook for 9 minutes, turning round halfway through cooking time.

Serve immediately, garnished with the parsley and accompanied by mashed potatoes and carrots.

Above: Beef, mushroom and onion suet pudding. Right: Chilli con carne; Beef bourguignon

CHILLI CON CARNE

Serves 4-6 Cooking time: 17 minutes
Microwave setting: Maximum (Full)

1 large onion, peeled and finely chopped
1 garlic clove, peeled and crushed
2 teaspoons tomato paste
30 g (1 oz) butter, cut into pieces
2 tablespoons plain flour
1 teaspoon chopped oregano
½ teaspoon ground cumin
2 teaspoons Mexican chilli powder
1×410 g can tomatoes, chopped with their juice
500 g (1 lb) minced beef
1×440 g can red kidney beans, drained
salt
freshly ground black pepper

Place the onion, garlic and tomato paste in a large bowl. Cover and cook for 5 minutes.

Stir in the butter until melted. Stir in the flour, oregano, cumin, chilli powder, undrained tomatoes and beef. Cook uncovered for 8 minutes. Stir and break up with a fork halfway through cooking.

Stir in the beans and cook uncovered for 4 minutes, stirring halfway through cooking.

Season to taste with salt and pepper and serve with boiled rice.

BEEF BOURGUIGNON

Serves 6 Cooking time: 65-75 minutes, plus standing
Microwave setting: Maximum (Full) and Defrost

2 medium onions, peeled and chopped
2 bacon rashers, rinds removed and chopped
185 g (6 oz) mushrooms, sliced
750 g (1½ lb) beef topside, cubed
2 tablespoons plain flour
1 cup red wine
⅓ cup hot beef stock
2 garlic cloves, peeled and crushed
2 teaspoons chopped, mixed herbs
freshly ground black pepper
salt

Place the onions and bacon in a large bowl, cover and cook on Maximum for 4 minutes.

Stir in the mushrooms and beef, cover and cook on Maximum for 7 minutes, stirring halfway through.

Stir in the flour, red wine, stock, garlic, herbs and pepper. Cover and cook on Maximum for 4 minutes, stirring halfway through, then switch to Defrost and cook for 50-60 minutes until fork-tender, seasoning with salt toward the end of cooking.

Leave to stand, covered, for 10 minutes.

BEEF WITH CHEESE SAUCE

Serves 4 Cooking time: 23 minutes
Microwave setting: Maximum (Full)

1 onion, peeled and thinly sliced
1 medium carrot, peeled and sliced
1 medium potato, peeled and sliced
125 g (4 oz) mushrooms, chopped
1 tablespoon tomato paste
375 g (12 oz) minced beef
2 teaspoons chopped, mixed herbs
freshly ground black pepper
salt
45 g (1½ oz) butter
3 tablespoons plain flour
2½ cups milk
1 cup finely grated Cheddar cheese
paprika (optional)

Place the onion, carrot and potato in a 6-cup heatproof dish. Cover and cook for 4½ minutes, stirring halfway through cooking.

Stir in the mushrooms, tomato paste, beef, herbs and pepper. Cover and cook for 8 minutes. Break up and stir with a fork halfway through. Salt to taste and set aside, covered.

Place the butter in a large bowl and cook uncovered for 30 seconds or until melted. Stir in the flour, cook 1 minute, then gradually blend in the milk, with salt and pepper to taste. Cook uncovered for 7 minutes or until thick, stirring every 2 minutes.

Stir in the cheese until melted. Pour the sauce over the beef mixture. Cook uncovered for 2 minutes and sprinkle with paprika, **or brown under a preheated conventional grill, if preferred.**

Below: Beef with cheese sauce.
Right: Chinese style beef; Mexican beef

CHINESE STYLE BEEF

Serves 4-6 Cooking time: 12 minutes, plus standing
Microwave setting: Maximum (Full)

1 tablespoon sesame oil
2 medium onions, peeled and sliced
1 red pepper, cored, seeded and thinly sliced
1 garlic clove, peeled and crushed
600 g (1¼ lb) fillet steak, cut into strips, 8×1 cm (3 inches×½ inch)
125 g (4 oz) button mushrooms, sliced
1 teaspoon ground ginger
¼ teaspoon ground cumin
¼ teaspoon grated nutmeg
1 tablespoon cornflour
¼ cup dry sherry
1 tablespoon lemon juice
¾ cup hot beef stock
1 tablespoon Worcestershire sauce
1 tablespoon soy sauce
freshly ground black pepper
1 cup bean sprouts
salt

Place the oil, onions, red pepper and garlic in a large bowl. Cover and cook for 5 minutes, stirring halfway through. Stir in the beef, mushrooms, ginger, cumin and nutmeg. Cover and cook for 3 minutes.

Stir in the cornflour blended with sherry, the lemon juice, stock, Worcestershire sauce, soy sauce and pepper to taste. Fold in the bean sprouts. Cover and cook for 4 minutes, stirring halfway through. Season with salt and leave to stand, covered, for 4 minutes before serving.

Serve with boiled rice.

MEXICAN BEEF

Serves 4-6 Cooking time: about 46 minutes, plus standing
Microwave setting: Maximum (Full) and Medium (½ power)

1 medium onion, peeled and sliced
1 small carrot, peeled and sliced
1 green pepper, cored, seeded and chopped
1 red pepper, cored, seeded and chopped
1 medium potato, peeled and diced
60 g (2 oz) butter, cut into pieces
2 teaspoons chopped oregano
1 teaspoon Mexican chilli powder
½ teaspoon Worcestershire sauce
1 tablespoon chopped parsley
1 garlic clove, peeled and crushed
600 g (1¼ lb) topside beef, cut into strips
2 tablespoons plain flour
freshly ground black pepper
1×410 g can tomatoes, chopped with their juice
½ cup hot beef stock
salt

Place the fresh vegetables in a large bowl. Cover and cook on Maximum for 2 minutes.

Stir in the butter until melted. Stir in the remaining ingredients except tomatoes, stock and salt. Cover and cook for 4 minutes, stirring halfway through.

Stir in the tomatoes and stock. Cover and cook on Medium for 40 minutes or until fork-tender, stirring halfway through and adding salt toward the end of cooking. Leave to stand, covered, for 5 minutes.

Steak oriental; Steak in pepper sauce

STEAK ORIENTAL

Serves 4 Cooking time: 12-14 minutes
Microwave setting: Maximum (Full)

4 fillet steaks, 2.5 cm (1 inch) thick, total weight 500 g (1 lb)
1 small celery stick, chopped
½ green pepper, cored, seeded and chopped
½ red pepper, cored, seeded and chopped
1 garlic clove, peeled and crushed
2 tablespoons tomato paste
2 teaspoons cornflour
3 tablespoons dry sherry
2 tablespoons soy sauce
6 canned water chestnuts, drained and sliced
salt
freshly ground black pepper

Place the steaks in a preheated, greased browning casserole. Cook uncovered for 3-5 minutes, depending on how rare you like your steak, and turning over and rearranging halfway through cooking. Set aside, covered, while making sauce.

Place the celery, peppers, garlic and tomato paste in a medium bowl. Cover and cook for 5 minutes, stirring halfway through cooking.

Stir in the cornflour blended with sherry, the soy sauce, water chestnuts, and salt and pepper to taste. Add any juice from the cooked steaks.

Pour the mixture over the steaks. Cover and cook for 4 minutes.

STEAK IN PEPPER SAUCE

Serves 4 Cooking time: 11½ minutes, plus standing
Microwave setting: Maximum (Full)

1 medium onion, peeled and finely chopped
60 g (2 oz) butter
1 garlic clove, peeled and crushed
1½ tablespoons cornflour
½ cup milk
1¼ cups hot beef stock
½ teaspoon freshly ground black pepper
6 black peppercorns
2 teaspoons green peppercorns
salt
4 sirloin steaks, total weight 750 g (1½ lb)

Place the onion, butter and garlic in a medium bowl. Cover and cook for 2 minutes.

Stir in the cornflour blended with milk, the hot stock and pepper. Crush 6 of the black peppercorns and add them to the sauce with the green peppercorns and salt.

Cover and cook for 2 minutes, stirring halfway through cooking. Leave covered and set aside.

Place the steaks in a preheated browning casserole. Cook for 3 minutes. Turn the steaks over and turn the casserole round. Cook for a further 2½ minutes.

Stir any meat juices into the sauce. Pour the sauce over the steaks, cover and cook for 2 minutes.

Leave to stand, covered, for 3 minutes before serving. Serve with a mixed salad.

Whisky steak; Steak with mushroom sauce

WHISKY STEAK

Serves 4 Cooking time: 12 minutes
Microwave setting: Maximum (Full)

4 rump steaks, total weight 750 g (1½ lb), lightly beaten
2 tablespoons whisky
1 garlic clove, peeled and crushed
1 medium onion, peeled and finely chopped
60 g (2 oz) butter
½ teaspoon Worcestershire sauce
freshly ground black pepper
green shallots, to garnish

Marinate the steaks in the whisky for 2 hours.

Place the garlic and onion in a large bowl. Cook, covered, for 2 minutes. Stir in the butter and cook uncovered for 30 seconds. Set aside.

Drain the steaks, reserving the marinade. Dry the steaks and place in a preheated, greased browning casserole. Cook uncovered for 7 minutes, turning over and rearranging halfway through cooking.

Pour the juice from the steaks into the butter mixture. Stir in the Worcestershire sauce, whisky from the marinade and pepper to taste.

Pour the sauce over the steaks and cook uncovered for 2½ minutes.

Garnish with green shallots and serve with plain boiled rice and a green vegetable.

STEAK WITH MUSHROOM SAUCE

Serves 4 Cooking time: 21 minutes
Microwave setting: Maximum (Full)

1 celery stick, chopped
1 onion, peeled and studded with 3 cloves
1 carrot, peeled and sliced
1¾ cups milk
4 thin sirloin steaks, total weight 750 g (1½ lb)
185 g (6 oz) mushrooms, sliced
60 g (2 oz) butter, cut into pieces
3 tablespoons plain flour
about ½ cup hot chicken stock
salt
freshly ground black pepper
parsley sprig, to garnish

Place the celery, onion, carrot and milk in a large bowl. Cook uncovered for 3 minutes. Set aside to infuse for 15 minutes.

Place the steaks in a preheated browning casserole and cook uncovered for 6 minutes, turning over and rearranging halfway through. Set aside, covered.

Place the mushrooms in a medium bowl, cover and cook for 3 minutes. Stir in the butter until melted. Add the flour and cook 1 minute. Make up the meat juices to ½ cup with the stock, then stir in with the strained milk, and salt and pepper to taste. Cook, uncovered, for 5 minutes, stirring every minute.

Pour the sauce over the steaks. Cook uncovered for 3 minutes. Garnish with the parsley.

MEATBALLS IN MUSHROOM & TOMATO SAUCE

Serves 4 Cooking time: 16 minutes
Microwave setting: Maximum (Full)

500 g (1 lb) minced beef
½ cup fresh brown breadcrumbs
1 onion, peeled and grated
2 teaspoons chopped thyme
1 tablespoon tomato paste
salt
freshly ground black pepper
1 egg

Sauce:
45 g (1½ oz) butter
125 g (4 oz) mushrooms, finely chopped
375 g (12 oz) tomatoes, skinned and chopped
1 tablespoon tomato paste
3 tablespoons plain flour
1¾ cups hot beef stock
salt
freshly ground black pepper

Mix the beef, breadcrumbs, onion, thyme, tomato paste, salt and pepper together. Add the egg and mix well. Form the mixture into 16 balls.

Place the meatballs in one layer in a preheated, greased browning casserole and cook for 2 minutes. Turn the meatballs over and turn the dish round. Cook for a further 2 minutes.

To make the sauce, place the butter, mushrooms, tomatoes and tomato paste in a medium bowl. Cover and cook for 5 minutes. Stir in the flour, then gradually add the hot stock. Cook for 2 minutes. Cool slightly.

Pour into a blender and blend until smooth. Stir in the salt and pepper.

Pour the sauce over meatballs. Cook for 5 minutes. Serve with noodles and Parmesan cheese.

BEEFBURGER & ONION ROLLS

Serves 4 Cooking time: 10¾ minutes
Microwave setting: Maximum (Full)

1 medium onion, peeled and sliced
1 medium onion, peeled and grated
250 g (8 oz) minced beef
1 garlic clove, peeled and crushed
2 teaspoons chopped, mixed herbs
salt
freshly ground black pepper
2 tablespoons plain flour
4 soft rolls, cut in half
lettuce and tomatoes, to garnish

Place the sliced onion in a medium bowl. Cover and cook for 4 minutes. Set aside.

Place the grated onion in another medium bowl. Cover and cook for 1 minute.

Stir in the minced beef, garlic, herbs, salt, pepper and flour, divide into 4 and shape into patties.

Place on a preheated, greased browning dish and cook for 3 minutes. Turn the beefburgers over and turn the dish round. Cook for a further 2 minutes.

Place a few cooked onion slices on 4 of the roll halves. Top with a beefburger, then the other half roll.

Place on a plate and cook for 45 seconds. Garnish with lettuce and tomatoes.

SAVOURY MINCE WITH MIXED VEGETABLES

Serves 4 Cooking time: 17 minutes
Microwave setting: Maximum (Full)

1 large potato, peeled and diced
1 turnip, peeled and diced
1 carrot, peeled and sliced
1 medium onion, peeled and sliced
1 celery stick, chopped
500 g (1 lb) minced beef
1 tablespoon chopped parsley
2 teaspoons soy sauce
¼ cup hot beef stock
¼ cup red wine
freshly ground black pepper
salt

Place the potato, turnip, carrot, onion and celery in a large bowl. Cover and cook for 10 minutes.

Stir in the remaining ingredients except salt. Cover and cook for 7 minutes, stirring and seasoning with salt halfway through cooking.

Serve with mashed potatoes.

Left: Meatballs in mushroom and tomato sauce; Beefburger and onion rolls.
Above: Savoury mince with mixed vegetables; Tomato cottage pie

TOMATO COTTAGE PIE

Serves 4 Cooking time: 23 minutes
Microwave setting: Maximum (Full)

750 g (1½ lb) potatoes, peeled and cut into 1 cm (½ inch) cubes
3 tablespoons water
1 medium onion, peeled and chopped
2 tablespoons tomato paste
2 tomatoes, skinned and chopped
500 g (1 lb) cooked beef, finely chopped
2 teaspoons chopped, mixed herbs
45 g (1½ oz) butter
½ teaspoon celery salt
½ cup hot beef stock
freshly ground black pepper
2-3 tablespoons milk
salt
paprika

Place the potatoes in a large bowl with the water. Cover and cook for 12 minutes, stirring halfway through cooking. Leave to stand, covered, while cooking the meat filling.

Place the onion in a 5-cup casserole dish, cover and cook for 3 minutes. Stir in the tomato paste, the chopped tomatoes, the beef, herbs, 30 g (1 oz) of the butter, the celery salt, stock and pepper to taste. Cover and cook for 4 minutes. Stir.

Meanwhile, mash the potatoes with the milk and remaining butter and season with salt and pepper to taste. Using a piping bag fitted with a large star nozzle, pipe the potato over the meat. Sprinkle lightly with paprika and cook uncovered for 4 minutes.

SHEPHERD'S PIE

Serves 4-5 Cooking time: 24 minutes
Microwave setting: Maximum (Full)

1 kg (2 lb) potatoes, peeled and cut into 2.5 cm (1 inch) cubes
3 tablespoons water
1 medium onion, peeled and thinly sliced
600 g (1¼ lb) minced beef
2 tablespoons tomato paste
1 teaspoon chopped parsley
½ teaspoon chopped oregano
½ teaspoon chopped marjoram
¼ teaspoon chopped sage
1 teaspoon Worcestershire sauce
freshly ground black pepper
salt
4 tablespoons milk
30 g (1 oz) butter
paprika (optional)
parsley sprig, to garnish

Place the potatoes and water in a large bowl, cover and cook for 12 minutes. Stir once during cooking. Set aside, covered, while cooking the beef.

Place the onion in a large shallow dish. Cover and cook for 2 minutes. Stir in the beef, tomato paste, herbs, Worcestershire sauce and pepper. Cover and cook for 6 minutes. Stir halfway through.

Drain off the excess liquid and season with salt.

Mash the potatoes with the milk, butter and salt and pepper to taste. Spread over the beef mixture and mark with a fork. Sprinkle with paprika, if using, and cook for 4 minutes or omit paprika and **brown under a preheated conventional grill.** Garnish with parsley.

MEAT LOAF

Serves 4-6 Cooking time: 12-15 minutes
Microwave setting: Maximum (Full)

1 medium onion, peeled and finely chopped
250 g (8 oz) minced pork
250 g (8 oz) minced beef
1 garlic clove, peeled and crushed
7 tablespoons fresh white breadcrumbs
1 tablespoon tomato paste
¼ teaspoon celery salt
2 teaspoons chopped parsley
1 teaspoon chopped thyme
salt
freshly ground black pepper
1 egg, beaten

Mix all ingredients together and pack into a greased souffle dish, non-metal loaf pan or ring mould.

Cook uncovered for 6 minutes. Break up and stir with a fork. If using a loaf pan, protect corners with small pieces of aluminium foil. Cook uncovered a further 4-6 minutes.

Serve hot or cold, sliced. If serving hot, top loaf with a mixture of 2 tablespoons each of Worcestershire sauce and grated cheese, and ⅓ cup of tomato sauce. Heat 2-3 minutes.

Meat loaf; Shepherd's pie

ROAST LUNCH

Rollmops

Roast Beef
Boiled Potatoes
Green Beans
Gravy

Trifle

Order of cooking:
Make the Rollmops (page 25) and Trifle (page 124) in advance.
Cook the beef.
While it is standing, cook the potatoes (page 105) and leave to stand while cooking the green beans (page 105).
Leave the beans to stand while making the gravy.

Gravy; Roast beef; Boiled potatoes; Green beans; Trifle; Rollmops

ROAST BEEF

Serves 6 Cooking time: 50 minutes, plus standing
Microwave setting: Maximum (Full) and Medium (½ power)

1×1.5 kg (3 lb) joint of yearling topside

Place the meat on a preheated browning dish and cover with paper towels. Cook for 10 minutes on Maximum, then 40 minutes on Medium, turning several times.

Tent the meat loosely with foil, shiny side inwards, and stand for 20 minutes.

Pour juices into a bowl, skim fat and use for gravy.

GRAVY

Makes about 1½ cups Cooking time: about 2 minutes
Microwave setting: Maximum (Full)

2 tablespoons cold water
2 teaspoons arrowroot
2 tablespoons meat juices
½ cup red wine
½ cup hot beef stock
dash Parisian essence
salt

Blend the water and arrowroot in a bowl. Add the remaining ingredients, salting to taste.

Cook uncovered for 2 minutes, stirring twice.

Roast leg of lamb

LAMB

ROAST LEG OF LAMB

Serves 4-6 Cooking time: 21 minutes, plus standing
Microwave setting: Maximum (Full)

1.5 kg (3 lb) leg of lamb

Wrap a small piece of foil around the thin end of the leg. Place the lamb, meaty side down, on a preheated browning dish.

Cover with paper towels and cook for 21 minutes, turning over several times.

Remove the lamb and tent loosely with foil, shiny side inward. Leave the covered lamb to stand for 20 minutes before carving.

Serve with mint sauce, potatoes (see page 15) and vegetables.

LAMB CHOPS WITH SPICY SAUCE

Serves 4 Cooking time: 10-11 minutes
Microwave setting: Maximum (Full)

1 small onion, peeled and finely sliced
60 g (2 oz) butter
4 lamb chump chops
1 tablespoon brown sugar
1 teaspoon Worcestershire sauce
1 teaspoon soy sauce
1 garlic clove, peeled and crushed
2 tablespoons tomato paste
salt
freshly ground black pepper

Place the onion and butter in a small bowl. Cover and cook for 2 minutes.

Place the chops in a preheated browning casserole. Cook for 5 minutes, turning once. Check if cooked to taste. Cook for 1 more minute if necessary. Pour off the meat juices and skim fat.

While the chops are cooking, mix the onion and butter with the remaining ingredients. Stir in the meat juices.

Spoon the sauce over the chops in the casserole, cover and cook for a further 3 minutes.

Serve with boiled rice and sweetcorn.

LAMB WITH CHERRIES

Serves 4 Cooking time: 20½ minutes
Microwave setting: Maximum (Full)

750 g (1½ lb) lamb fillets
1 tablespoon oil
1 medium onion, peeled and chopped
30 g (1 oz) butter, cut into pieces
500 g (1 lb) fresh cherries, stoned, or 1×860 g can cherries, drained and rinsed
1 teaspoon chopped marjoram
salt
about 1 cup hot chicken stock
1 tablespoon cornflour
2 tablespoons water

Brush the fillets with oil and place in a preheated, browning casserole. Cook uncovered for 6½ minutes, turning once. Remove fillets, cover and keep warm. Pour off meat juices and reserve.

Place the onion in the casserole, cover and cook for 3 minutes. Stir in the butter until melted. Stir in the cherries, marjoram and a little salt, cover and cook 3 minutes for fresh cherries, 1 minute for canned.

Make up the meat juices to 1 cup with the stock and stir in blended cornflour and water, then stir into the onion and cherries. Cook uncovered for 5 minutes, stirring occasionally.

Arrange the fillets in a shallow serving dish and spoon over the sauce. Cook, uncovered, 3 minutes.

Clockwise: Lamb with Mozzarella cheese; Sweet and sour lamb; Lamb with cherries; Lamb chops with spicy sauce

LAMB WITH MOZZARELLA CHEESE

Serves 4 Cooking time: 6-7 minutes
Microwave setting: Maximum (Full)

8 lamb cutlets
125 g (4 oz) Mozzarella cheese, thinly sliced
1 tablespoon chopped parsley, to garnish

Marinade:
2 tablespoons white wine vinegar
½ cup dry sherry
2 teaspoons brown sugar
1 tablespoon orange juice
¼ teaspoon Worcestershire sauce
salt
freshly ground black pepper

Mix together the vinegar, sherry, sugar, orange juice, Worcestershire sauce and salt and pepper.

Arrange the cutlets in a shallow dish. Pour over the marinade and add sufficient cold water to cover the cutlets. Leave to marinate for about 24 hours.

Drain the marinade off the cutlets. Cover the cutlets with a piece of paper towel. Cook for 4-5 minutes, rearranging halfway through cooking.

Pour off the juice and arrange the cutlets close together. Cover them with the cheese and cook, uncovered, for 2 minutes.

Sprinkle with chopped parsley to garnish.

SWEET & SOUR LAMB

Serves 4 Cooking time: 19 minutes
Microwave setting: Maximum (Full)

4 lamb loin chops, total weight 600 g (1¼ lb)
1 medium onion, peeled and chopped
½ green pepper, cored, seeded and finely chopped
½ red pepper, cored, seeded and finely chopped
1 teaspoon grated fresh ginger
2 teaspoons chopped parsley
1 garlic clove, peeled and crushed
30 g (1 oz) butter, cut into pieces
2 tablespoons plain flour
1¼ cups hot chicken stock
2 tablespoons white wine vinegar
1 tablespoon soy sauce
⅓ cup brown sugar
salt
freshly ground black pepper

Place the chops in a preheated browning casserole, cover with a paper towel and cook for 7 minutes, turning over and rearranging halfway through cooking. Set aside, covered.

Place the onion, peppers, ginger, parsley and garlic in a medium bowl. Cover and cook for 5 minutes, stirring halfway through.

Stir in the butter until melted. Stir in the flour and cook 1 minute. Pour off meat juices from the chops, skim fat and make up to 1¼ cups with the stock. Blend into the vegetables with the remaining ingredients. Cook uncovered for 3 minutes, stirring every minute.

Pour the sauce over the chops and cook uncovered for 3 minutes.

Serve with buttered noodles.

CROWN ROAST OF LAMB

Serves 4-6 Cooking time: 29-34 minutes, plus standing
Microwave setting: Maximum (Full)

1 medium onion, peeled and finely chopped
60 g (2 oz) butter, cut into pieces
1 garlic clove, peeled and crushed
meat trimmings (from preparing lamb), finely chopped
2 cups fresh white breadcrumbs
½ teaspoon chopped marjoram
¼ teaspoon chopped rosemary
1 teaspoon chopped parsley
¼ teaspoon celery salt
freshly ground black pepper
1 egg, lightly beaten
2 skinned racks of lamb, total prepared weight 1-1.25 kg (2-2½ lb), comprising 12-14 cutlets
12-14 glace cherries, to garnish

Bend each skinned rack into a semi-circle, fat inwards, cutting between but not dividing chops, if necessary. Sew ends together to form a circle.

Place the onion, butter, garlic and meat trimmings in a medium bowl. Cover and cook for 4 minutes. Stir in the remaining ingredients except cherries.

Stuff the centre of the roast and stand on a microwave roasting rack or upturned saucer on a plate. Cook uncovered for 25-30 minutes, turning round halfway through cooking.

Tent loosely with foil and stand for 20-25 minutes. Place a cherry on top of each bone to garnish.

LAMB IN CREAM & CIDER

Serves 4 Cooking time: about 18½ minutes
Microwave setting: Maximum (Full)

8 lamb loin chops, total weight 1 kg (2 lb), trimmed of skin and excess fat
1 medium onion, peeled and chopped
250 g (8 oz) mushrooms, sliced
½ teaspoon chopped rosemary
30 g (1 oz) butter, softened
2 tablespoons plain flour
about ⅓ cup hot chicken stock
1 cup dry cider
salt
freshly ground black pepper
4 tablespoons cream
chopped parsley, to garnish

Place the chops around the bottom and sides of a large bowl, cover and cook for 6½ minutes, rearranging halfway through. Set aside, covered.

Place the onion in a large bowl, cover and cook for 4 minutes. Stir in the mushrooms and rosemary, blend butter and flour and stir in. Cover and cook for 3 minutes.

Make up the defatted meat juices to ⅓ cup with the stock, then stir in with the cider and salt and pepper. Add the chops. Cover and cook for 4 minutes, stirring halfway through.

Skim if necessary, then stir in the cream and reheat for 1 minute if necessary. Sprinkle with chopped parsley, to garnish.

Crown roast of lamb; Lamb in cream and cider

LAMB CURRY

Serves 4-6 Cooking time: 13 minutes
Microwave setting: Maximum (Full)

30 g (1 oz) ghee
1 medium onion, peeled and chopped
1 garlic clove, peeled and crushed
1 tablespoon ground coriander
1 teaspoon turmeric
½ teaspoon ground cumin
¼ teaspoon cinnamon
¼ teaspoon ground ginger
¼ teaspoon grated nutmeg
1 tablespoon plain flour
1 tablespoon tomato paste
1 teaspoon lemon juice
1 tablespoon desiccated coconut
2 tablespoons sultanas
1¾ cups hot beef stock
2 teaspoons curry paste
750 g (1½ lb) boneless cooked lamb, finely chopped
freshly ground black pepper
salt

Place the ghee, onion, garlic and spices in a large bowl. Cover and cook for 2 minutes.

Stir in the flour and cook 1 minute. Add the tomato paste, lemon juice, coconut, sultanas, stock, curry paste, lamb and pepper. Cover and cook for 10 minutes, stirring twice and seasoning with salt the second time.

Serve with rice, sliced tomatoes, sliced bananas, mango chutney and desiccated coconut.

MOUSSAKA

Serves 4-6 Cooking time: about 34 minutes
Microwave setting: Maximum (Full)

1 large eggplant, cut into 5 mm (¼ inch) slices
salt
2 tablespoons oil
30 g (1 oz) butter
2 medium onions, peeled and finely sliced
2 garlic cloves, peeled and crushed
500 g (1 lb) lamb, minced
2 tablespoons plain flour
3 tablespoons tomato paste
½ cup beef stock
freshly ground black pepper
chopped parsley, to garnish

Sauce:
30 g (1 oz) butter
2 tablespoons plain flour
1¼ cups milk
½ cup grated Cheddar cheese
1 teaspoon dry mustard
1 egg, beaten

Sprinkle eggplant slices with salt, stand 30 minutes, rinse and dry. Brush slices with oil and cook on a preheated browning dish for 3 minutes, turning once.

Place the butter, onions and garlic in a large bowl. Cover and cook for 4 minutes. Stir in the lamb and flour, cover and cook for 4 minutes. Stir in the tomato paste, stock and pepper. Cover, cook for 12 minutes. Season with salt.

To make the sauce, place the butter in a bowl. Cook for ¾ minute or until melted. Blend in the flour and cook 1 minute. Stir in the milk. Cook for 2½ minutes, stirring twice. Stir in the cheese, mustard and egg.

Make layers of lamb and eggplant slices in a shallow casserole, cook 4 minutes. Pour over the sauce and cook for 4 minutes or until set. Sprinkle with parsley.

Lamb curry; Moussaka

STUFFED LEG OF LAMB

Serves 4-6 Cooking time: 18-22 minutes, plus standing
Microwave setting: Maximum (Full)

- 1 small onion, peeled and finely chopped
- 30 g (1 oz) butter
- 1½ cups fresh white breadcrumbs
- 2 teaspoons chopped thyme
- salt
- freshly ground black pepper
- 1 egg, beaten
- 1 kg (2 lb) boned leg of lamb

Place the onion and butter in a large bowl. Cover and cook for 2 minutes. Stir in the breadcrumbs, thyme, salt, pepper and egg.

Lay the boned leg of lamb out flat. Spread the stuffing over the meat, roll up and tie with string. Place lamb, fat side down, on a preheated browning dish and cover with paper towels. Cook for 16-20 minutes, turning twice. Tent the meat loosely with foil and stand for 15 minutes. If liked, serve with Gravy (page 55).

STUFFED LOIN OF LAMB

Serves 4-5 Cooking time: 11-13 minutes, plus standing
Microwave setting: Maximum (Full)

- 1 medium onion, peeled and chopped
- 30 g (1 oz) butter
- 2 cups fresh white breadcrumbs
- ½ teaspoon chopped rosemary
- grated rind of 1 orange
- 1 tablespoon orange juice
- salt
- freshly ground black pepper
- 500 g (1 lb) boned loin of lamb

Place the onion and butter in a medium bowl, cover and cook for 3 minutes. Stir in the remaining ingredients except lamb.

Spread the stuffing over the loin, roll up and tie with string. Place on a preheated browning dish, seam side upward, and cover with a paper towel. Cook uncovered for 8-10 minutes, turning once. Tent meat loosely with foil and stand 10 minutes. If liked, make Gravy (page 55), using orange juice instead of wine.

DINNER PARTY

Liver Pate

Guard of Honour
Vichy Carrots
Sweetcorn

Cold Strawberry Souffle

Order of cooking:

Make the pate (page 30) and souffle (page 120), and prepare the guard in advance.

Cook the Guard of Honour and while it is standing, cook the carrots (page 105).

Leave to stand while cooking the sweetcorn (page 105).

Left: Stuffed leg of lamb; Stuffed loin of lamb. Above: Guard of honour; Sweetcorn; Vichy carrots; Cold strawberry souffle; Liver pate

GUARD OF HONOUR

Serves 4 Cooking time: 25 minutes, plus standing
Microwave setting: Maximum (Full)

30 g (1 oz) butter
1 small onion, peeled and chopped
¼ teaspoon chopped marjoram
¼ teaspoon chopped rosemary
¼ teaspoon chopped sage
1 tablespoon chopped parsley
1½ cups fresh white breadcrumbs
salt
freshly ground black pepper
1 egg, beaten
1 guard of honour, prepared weight 750 g (1½ lb), each rack comprising 6 cutlets
Gravy (page 55)

To prepare guard:

Interlock bones of racks, push bases together and tie.

Place the butter, onion and herbs in a small bowl. Cover and cook for 3 minutes. Stir in the breadcrumbs, salt, pepper and egg.

Stuff the guard. Place on a microwave roasting rack or shallow dish. Cook for 22 minutes, turning round halfway through. Tent loosely with foil and stand for 15-20 minutes. Make Gravy (page 55), brush a little on the guard just before serving and serve the remainder separately.

Roast pork

PORK, BACON & HAM

ROAST PORK

Serves 4-6 Cooking time: 30 minutes, plus standing and grilling
Microwave setting: Maximum (Full)

1 × 1.5 kg (3 lb) top half leg of pork, skin scored	1 tablespoon oil
	½ teaspoon salt

If an exact 1.5 kg (3 lb) piece of pork is not available, check the chart on page 9 for cooking times per 500 g (1 lb).

Rub the oil into the pork skin, then rub in the salt. Place the meat on a preheated browning dish, fat downward, and cover with a paper towel. Cook for 30 minutes, turning twice.

Tent the meat loosely with foil, shiny side inward, and leave for 15-20 minutes before carving. If desired, **crisp skin under a preheated conventional grill.**

Serve with potatoes, peas, carrots, stuffing, Apple Sauce (page 139) and Gravy (page 55).

PORK CASSEROLE

Serves 4 Cooking time: 17-19 minutes
Microwave setting: Maximum (Full)

500 g (1 lb) pork fillet, cut into 2.5 cm (1 inch) pieces
1 onion, peeled and finely chopped
2 carrots, peeled and thinly sliced
1 red pepper, cored, seeded and chopped
1 garlic clove, peeled and crushed
¼ teaspoon ground mace
½ teaspoon chopped thyme
¼ teaspoon chopped sage
1 teaspoon chopped parsley
1½ tablespoons tomato paste
30 g (1 oz) butter, softened
2 tablespoons plain flour
about 1¼ cups chicken stock
1×310 g can sweetcorn kernels, drained
salt
freshly ground black pepper

Place the pork in a preheated browning casserole and cook uncovered for 4-6 minutes, stirring halfway through cooking. Set aside, covered.

Place the onion, carrots, red pepper, garlic, mace, herbs and tomato paste in a medium bowl. Cover and cook for 8 minutes, stirring halfway through.

Blend the butter and flour in a mixing bowl, stir in and cook for 1 minute. Pour off the juices from the pork and make up to 1¼ cups with stock, then stir in with the sweetcorn, salt and pepper. Pour the mixture over the pork and cook uncovered for 4 minutes, stirring every minute.

From left to right: Pork casserole; Pork chops with apple; Pork chops with oregano and tomato sauce

PORK CHOPS WITH APPLE

Serves 4 Cooking time: 9-11 minutes, plus standing
Microwave setting: Maximum (Full)

2 teaspoons soy sauce
2 teaspoons Worcestershire sauce
60 g (2 oz) butter
2 tablespoons brown sugar
salt
freshly ground black pepper
4 pork chops, total weight 750 g (1½ lb)
1 large eating apple, peeled, cored and cut into 4 slices

Place the soy sauce, Worcestershire sauce, butter, sugar, salt and pepper in a jug. Cook for 1 minute. Stir the sauce.

Brush both sides of the chops and apple slices with the sauce.

Arrange the pork chops in a preheated browning casserole. Cook uncovered for 4 minutes. Turn the chops over and rearrange.

Brush the chops with any remaining sauce and place a slice of apple on each one. Cover and cook for 4-6 minutes.

Leave to stand, covered, for 3 minutes.

PORK CHOPS WITH OREGANO & TOMATO SAUCE

Serves 4 Cooking time: 16-18 minutes
Microwave setting: Maximum (Full)

4 pork loin chops, total weight 750 g (1½ lb)
1 medium onion, peeled and finely chopped
1 teaspoon chopped oregano
30 g (1 oz) butter, cut into pieces
1 tablespoon cornflour
1×410 g can tomatoes with their juice
1 tablespoon tomato paste
1 tablespoon chopped parsley
¾ cup hot chicken stock
salt
freshly ground black pepper

Place the chops in a preheated browning casserole, cover with a paper towel and cook for 8 minutes. Turn over halfway through. Pour off fat, cover and set aside.

Place the onion and oregano in a large bowl, cover and cook for 2 minutes, stirring halfway through.

Stir in the butter until melted. Stir in the cornflour, then the remaining ingredients. Cover and cook for 3-5 minutes, stirring halfway through.

Add to chops. Cook uncovered for 3 minutes.

GARLIC BACON STICKS

Makes 8 Cooking time: 6-8 minutes
Microwave setting: Maximum (Full)

1 garlic clove
8 streaky bacon rashers, rinds removed and stretched
8 grissini (bread sticks)
¼ cup finely grated Cheddar cheese

Rub the garlic over each rasher of bacon.

Twist a rasher of bacon around the top half of each bread stick. Place the sticks on a paper towel on a plate. Cook, covered with a paper towel, for 6-8 minutes or until the bacon is cooked.

Twirl the hot bacon in the cheese to coat on all sides. Serve hot or cold with drinks.

Glazed bacon joint; Garlic bacon sticks

GLAZED BACON JOINT

Serves 4-6 Cooking time: 50½ minutes, plus standing and grilling
Microwave setting: Maximum (Full) and Medium (½ power)

1.5 kg (3 lb) piece boiling bacon, soaked overnight and drained
2 tablespoons marmalade

Remove bacon skin and place the bacon in a roasting bag. Tie with string and prick the bag. Place in a shallow dish and cook on Maximum 10 minutes. Turn over and cook on Medium a further 40 minutes.

Remove bacon from bag, wrap tightly in foil and stand for 15 minutes.

Heat the marmalade in a small bowl for 30 seconds. Place the bacon in a grill pan and spread the marmalade over. **Cook under a preheated conventional grill until bubbling.**

PORK WITH ORANGE & CRANBERRIES

Serves 4-6 Cooking time: about 17 minutes
Microwave setting: Maximum (Full)

4 pork fillets, total weight 750 g (1½ lb)
2 teaspoons oil
grated rind of 1 orange
¼ cup orange juice
1 tablespoon caster sugar
1×454 g can cranberries, drained
4 orange slices, to garnish

Brush the fillets with oil, place in a preheated browning dish, cover with a paper towel and cook for 6 minutes, turning over halfway through. Set aside, covered.

Place the orange rind and juice, sugar and cranberries in a medium bowl. Cover and cook for 2½ minutes. Stir, re-cover and cook for 5½ minutes on Defrost.

Drain the fillets and spoon the cranberry mixture over them. Cook uncovered for 3 minutes.

Cut into slices and garnish with orange.

Pork with orange and cranberries;
Pork fillets in wine sauce

PORK FILLETS IN WINE SAUCE

Serves 4-6 Cooking time: 18-21 minutes
Microwave setting: Maximum (Full)

4 pork fillets, total weight 750 g (1½ lb)
2 teaspoons oil
1 medium onion, peeled and chopped
125 g (4 oz) button mushrooms, sliced
1 celery stick, sliced
1 teaspoon chopped parsley
¼ teaspoon chopped sage
½ teaspoon chopped tarragon
30 g (1 oz) butter, diced
2 tablespoons plain flour
about ½ cup hot chicken stock
½ cup rosé wine
salt
freshly ground black pepper

To garnish:
fried apple rings

Brush the fillets with oil, place in a preheated browning dish and cover with a paper towel. Cook for 6-9 minutes, turning over halfway through cooking. Set aside, covered.

Place the vegetables and herbs in a medium bowl. Cover and cook for 4 minutes.

Stir in the butter until melted. Stir in the flour and cook 1 minute. Pour off juices from the pork and make up to ½ cup with stock, then stir in with the wine, salt and pepper. Cook, covered, for 4 minutes, stirring after 1 minute. Pour over the fillets and cook, covered, 3 minutes. Garnish with apple.

HAM IN CIDER

Serves 4-6 Cooking time: about 15 minutes
Microwave setting: Maximum (Full)

600 g (1¼ lb) ham, cubed
1 medium onion, peeled and chopped
1 celery stick, chopped
1 teaspoon chopped marjoram
2 red eating apples, cored and sliced
30 g (1 oz) butter, softened
2 tablespoons cornflour
½ cup hot chicken stock
1¼ cups dry cider
freshly ground black pepper

Place the ham in a shallow dish, cover and cook for 4 minutes, stirring halfway through cooking. Remove the ham with its juices and set aside, covered.

Add the onion, celery and marjoram to the dish, cover and cook for 3 minutes.

Stir in the apples, cover and cook for 2 minutes.

Stir in the butter blended with cornflour, the stock, cider and pepper to taste. Cook uncovered for 3 minutes or until thickened, stirring every minute.

Replace ham and its juices. Heat through about 3 minutes. Serve with new potatoes and broccoli.

BACON & VEGETABLE CASSEROLE

Serves 4 Cooking time: 20 minutes
Microwave setting: Maximum (Full)

½ green pepper, cored, seeded and thinly sliced
2 onions, peeled and thinly sliced into rings
2 medium potatoes, peeled and diced
1 celery stick, chopped
1 carrot, peeled and thinly sliced
125 g (4 oz) frozen cauliflower florets
12 streaky bacon rashers, rinds removed, stretched, rolled and secured with wooden toothpicks
2 tablespoons plain flour
1¾ cups hot chicken stock
salt
freshly ground black pepper

Place the vegetables in a large bowl. Cover and cook for 9 minutes, stirring twice during the cooking time.

Place the bacon rolls in a casserole, cover with a paper towel and cook for 5 minutes.

Remove the bacon. Stir in the flour and cook 1 minute. Stir in the stock and salt and pepper to taste. Cook for 3 minutes, stirring once.

Remove the toothpicks from the bacon rolls. Mix the bacon and vegetables with the sauce. Cook uncovered

for 2 minutes.

Serve immediately as a complete and filling supper dish.

Variation:
Use red or yellow peppers in place of the green pepper, and swede turnips or pumpkin in place of the carrots.

HAM STEAKS WITH PINEAPPLE

Serves 4 Cooking time: 11 minutes, plus standing
Microwave setting: Maximum (Full)

4 ham steaks, total weight 1 kg (2 lb)
4 slices of fresh or canned pineapple, drained and cut in half

Arrange the steaks over the bottom and sides of a large bowl. Cover and cook for 8 minutes, rearranging halfway through cooking.

Pour off the juice and arrange the steaks in a serving dish with the pineapple. Cook uncovered for 3 minutes.

Cover the dish with foil and stand for 4 minutes before serving. Serve with saute potatoes or rice.

From left to right: Ham in cider; Bacon and vegetable casserole; Ham steaks with pineapple

PAPRIKA PORK CHOPS

Serves 4 Cooking time: 15-18 minutes
Microwave setting: Maximum (Full)

4 pork rib chops, total weight 750 g (1½ lb)
½ green pepper, cored, seeded and sliced
½ red pepper, cored, seeded and sliced
1 celery stick, chopped
¼ teaspoon Worcestershire sauce
1 tablespoon tomato paste
1 tablespoon paprika
½ teaspoon chopped oregano
½ teaspoon chopped basil
30 g (1 oz) butter, softened
2 tablespoons cornflour
about 1¾ cups hot chicken stock
salt
freshly ground black pepper
2 tablespoons sour cream

Place the chops in a preheated browning dish and cook, covered with a paper towel, for 6-9 minutes, turning over and rearranging halfway. Set aside, covered.

Place the peppers, celery, Worcestershire sauce, tomato paste, paprika, oregano and basil in a medium bowl. Cover and cook for 5 minutes, stirring halfway through cooking.

Stir in the butter blended with the cornflour. Pour off meat juices, skim fat and make up to 1¾ cups with stock, then stir in with salt and pepper. Cook uncovered 2 minutes, stirring once. Pour over chops and cook uncovered 3 minutes. Stir in sour cream.

COLD CURRIED PORK

Serves 4 Cooking time: 5-7 minutes
Microwave setting: Maximum (Full)

500 g (1 lb) pork fillet, cubed
2 eating apples, cored and diced
2 green shallots, trimmed and chopped
½ red pepper, cored, seeded and chopped
½ small cucumber, peeled and diced
1 carrot, peeled and grated
2 tablespoons sultanas
2 tablespoons roasted peanuts
1 celery stick, chopped
1 tablespoon mild curry powder
1 cup mayonnaise
salt
freshly ground black pepper
green shallots, to garnish

Place the pork in a large bowl, cover and cook for 5-7 minutes, stirring halfway through cooking. Leave to stand, covered, until cold. Drain.

Mix together the apples, shallots, red pepper, cucumber, carrot, sultanas, peanuts and celery.

Mix together the curry powder, mayonnaise and salt and pepper to taste. Stir in the pork and the fruit and vegetable mixture. Chill, garnish with shallots.

Clockwise: Spareribs with barbecue sauce; Pork kebabs; Cold curried pork; Paprika pork chops

SPARERIBS WITH BARBECUE SAUCE

Serves 4 Cooking time: 28½-30½ minutes
Microwave setting: Maximum (Full)

750 g (1½ lb) pork spareribs
15 g (½ oz) butter
1 garlic clove, peeled and crushed
1 medium onion, peeled and finely chopped
1×410 g can tomatoes, drained
1 tablespoon chopped oregano
2 tablespoons Worcestershire sauce
1 tablespoon honey
1 tablespoon soy sauce
1 tablespoon brown sugar
salt
freshly ground black pepper

Place the spareribs in a preheated browning dish, cover with a paper towel and cook 4 minutes, turning once. Pour off fat and set aside.

Place the butter, garlic and onion in a bowl. Cover and cook 3½ minutes. Stir in remaining ingredients, cover and cook 5 minutes. Add to drained spareribs. Cover and cook 16-18 minutes, rearranging ribs once.

PORK KEBABS

Serves 4 Cooking time: 11 minutes
Microwave setting: Maximum (Full)

Marinade:
3 tablespoons olive oil
½ cup water
2 tablespoons Worcestershire sauce
1 small onion, peeled and sliced
1 tablespoon white wine vinegar
small piece bay leaf, crumbled
1 tablespoon redcurrant jelly
salt
freshly ground black pepper

Kebabs:
500 g (1 lb) pork fillet, cut into 4 cm (1½ inch) cubes
½ red pepper, cored, seeded and cut into 8 pieces
½ green pepper, cored, seeded and cut into 8 pieces
2 small tomatoes, halved

Sauce:
30 g (1 oz) butter
2 tablespoons plain flour
½ cup hot chicken stock
1 tablespoon tomato paste

Mix together the marinade ingredients, with salt and pepper to taste, in a shallow dish. Add the pork cubes and turn to coat. Leave for 2 hours.

Drain the pork cubes, reserving the marinade. Thread the pork cubes and pepper pieces alternately on to 4 wooden skewers. Place on a preheated browning dish and cover with paper towels. Cook for 3 minutes.

Turn skewers over. Place half a tomato on each, cover again and cook for 3 minutes. Set aside.

Place the butter in a bowl and cook uncovered for 1 minute or until melted. Stir in the flour and cook 1 minute. Blend in the strained, reserved marinade, hot chicken stock and tomato paste. Cook for 3 minutes, stirring every minute. Serve with kebabs.

PICNIC HAM PATE

Serves 4 Cooking time: 7½ minutes
Microwave setting: Maximum (Full)

60 g (2 oz) mushrooms
1 onion, peeled and quartered
375 g (12 oz) lean ham, roughly chopped
1 garlic clove, peeled
2 leaves sage
2 tablespoons parsley sprigs
few leaves rosemary
1 sprig marjoram
freshly ground black pepper
2 eggs, lightly beaten

To garnish:
lettuce
tomato slices

Process in a food processor or finely mince together the mushrooms, onion, ham, garlic, herbs and pepper to taste. Bind the mixture with the eggs.

Line a 15-16 cm (6-6½ inch) diameter souffle dish with plastic film and place an inexpensive tumbler upside down in the centre. Spread the ham mixture evenly in the dish.

Cover and cook for 7½ minutes, turning halfway through cooking. Leave to cool before turning out.

Garnish with lettuce and sliced tomatoes and serve with potato salad

FRANKFURTS WRAPPED IN BACON

Serves 4 Cooking time: 4 minutes
Microwave setting: Maximum (Full)

8 streaky bacon rashers, rinds removed
8 large frankfurts, slashed
parsley sprigs, to garnish

Wind the bacon round the frankfurts and secure with toothpicks. Place in a circle on a plate. Cover with a paper towel and cook for 4 minutes. Remove toothpicks, garnish with the parsley sprigs and serve with potato salad.

Left: Picnic ham pate; Frankfurts wrapped in bacon. Right, clockwise: Jellied ham and chicken; Baked bananas; Stuffed loin of pork; Croquette potatoes; Apple sauce; Broccoli with cheese sauce

DINNER PARTY

Jellied Ham and Chicken

Stuffed Pork Loin
Croquette Potatoes
Broccoli with Cheese Sauce
Apple Sauce

Baked Bananas

Order of cooking:

Earlier in the day, make the jellied ham and chicken (page 27), croquette potatoes (page 102) and apple sauce (page 139). Prepare the pork for cooking.

Cook the loin and while it is standing, cook the broccoli, the sauce (page 106), then the baked bananas (page 126).

Reheat the potatoes and apple sauce just before serving. They will take 3 minutes each, or 6 minutes if put in the oven together (but check the apple sauce and remove it as soon as it is hot).

STUFFED PORK LOIN

Serves 4-6 Cooking time: 23 minutes, plus grilling
Microwave setting: Maximum (Full) and Medium High (¾ power)

1 small onion, peeled and finely chopped
1 garlic clove, peeled and crushed
30 g (1 oz) butter
½ cup fresh white breadcrumbs
grated rind of 1 lemon
¼ teaspoon chopped rosemary
1 teaspoon chopped thyme
salt
freshly ground black pepper
1 × 1 kg (2 lb) boned loin of pork, skin scored

Place the onion, garlic and butter in a bowl. Cover and cook for 3 minutes. Stir in the breadcrumbs, lemon rind, rosemary, thyme, salt and pepper.

Spread the stuffing over the loin, roll up and tie with string. Place in a shallow dish, skin uppermost, and cook uncovered on Maximum for 10 minutes, turning round halfway through, then on Medium High for 10 minutes.

Tent loosely with foil and stand for 15-20 minutes before serving. If desired, **brown the loin under a preheated conventional grill.**

Devilled chicken drumsticks;
Turkey breasts Cordon bleu

POULTRY & GAME

DEVILLED CHICKEN DRUMSTICKS

Serves 3-4 Cooking time: 12½ minutes
Microwave setting: Maximum (Full)

750 g (1½ lb) chicken drumsticks
1 teaspoon curry powder
1 tablespoon soy sauce
2 tablespoons tomato paste
3 tablespoons brown sugar
30 g (1 oz) butter, cut into pieces
green shallots, to garnish

Place the drumsticks in one layer in a shallow casserole dish. Cook uncovered for 4½ minutes.

Place the curry powder, soy sauce, tomato paste, sugar and butter in a bowl. Cook uncovered for 1½ minutes.

Rearrange the drumsticks and brush with the sauce. Cook uncovered for 4½ minutes.

Brush the remaining sauce over the drumsticks and cook for 2 minutes. Garnish with shallots.

Serve with rice and a green salad.

TURKEY BREASTS CORDON BLEU

Serves 4 Cooking time: 7-9 minutes
Microwave setting: Maximum (Full)

4 skinless turkey fillets (schnitzels), total weight 400-500 g (14 oz-1 lb)
freshly ground black pepper
60 g (2 oz) butter, diced
4 slices of cooked ham
4 slices of Gruyere cheese
parsley sprigs, to garnish

Place the turkey in a shallow dish. Sprinkle with pepper and dot with butter. Cover and cook for 4-6 minutes, turning over and rearranging once.

Transfer to a serving plate. Top the fillets with ham, then cheese. Cook uncovered for 3 minutes, or *brown under a preheated conventional grill if preferred.* Garnish with parsley.

CHICKEN & PEPPERS

Serves 4 Cooking time: 26½-29½ minutes
Microwave setting: Maximum (Full)

4 skinned chicken pieces, total weight 1.25 kg (2½ lb)
1 carrot, peeled and sliced
1 medium onion, peeled and sliced
1 small red pepper, cored, seeded and sliced
1 small green pepper, cored, seeded and sliced
1 garlic clove, peeled and crushed
½ teaspoon chopped sage
1 tablespoon chopped parsley
2 tablespoons tomato paste
30 g (1 oz) butter, cut into pieces
about 1½ cups hot chicken stock
2 tablespoons cornflour
4 tablespoons water
salt
freshly ground black pepper

Place the chicken pieces round sides of a large bowl. Cover and cook for 9-12 minutes, rearranging halfway through. Set aside, covered.

Place the vegetables, herbs, tomato paste and butter in a large bowl. Cover and cook for 10 minutes, stirring halfway through.

Skim fat from chicken juices and make up to 1½ cups with stock. Stir in cornflour blended with water, then stir into vegetables with salt and pepper. Cook uncovered for 3½ minutes, stirring every minute.

Pour over the chicken and cook uncovered for 4 minutes. Serve with hot, fluffy rice.

CHICKEN LIVER & GRAPES

Serves 4-6 Cooking time: 14½ minutes
Microwave setting: Maximum (Full)

125 g (4 oz) butter
1 garlic clove, peeled and crushed
1 tablespoon tomato paste
1 tablespoon chopped parsley
30 g (1 oz) mushrooms, finely sliced
750 g (1½ lb) chicken livers, trimmed and chopped
375 g (12 oz) black grapes, halved and seeded
salt
freshly ground black pepper
1 tablespoon cornflour
½ cup red wine
chopped parsley, to garnish

Place the butter, garlic, tomato paste, parsley and mushrooms in a large bowl. Cover and cook for 2 minutes.

Stir in the livers. Cover and cook for 6 minutes. Stir in the grapes, salt and pepper. Cover and cook for 4 minutes.

Blend together the cornflour and wine, then stir into the livers. Cook uncovered for 2½ minutes, stirring halfway through cooking.

Garnish with the chopped parsley. Serve with rice.

CHICKEN MARENGO

Serves 4 Cooking time: about 28-29 minutes
Microwave setting: Maximum (Full)

1.25 kg (2½ lb) chicken pieces (half breasts, thighs, Marylands)
1 onion, peeled and finely chopped
6 tomatoes, skinned, seeded and chopped
185 g (6 oz) button mushrooms
1 garlic clove, peeled and crushed
½ teaspoon chopped rosemary
½ teaspoon chopped sage
30 g (1 oz) butter, cut into pieces
about ½ cup hot chicken stock
¼ cup white wine
1 tablespoon brandy
salt
freshly ground black pepper
fresh sage, to garnish

Place the chicken pieces, skin downward, in a preheated browning dish. Cover with a paper towel and cook for 10 minutes, turning once. Set aside.

Place the vegetables, herbs and butter in a bowl. Cover and cook for 8 minutes, stirring halfway through.

Skim fat from the chicken juices and make up to ½ cup with stock. Stir into the vegetables with the wine, brandy, salt and pepper. Cook for 3 minutes, stirring once.

Pour over the chicken and cook uncovered for 7-8 minutes or until chicken is tender. Garnish with sage.

COQ AU VIN

Serves 4 Cooking time: 50 minutes
Microwave setting: Maximum (Full) and Defrost

1.25 kg (2½ lb) chicken pieces (half breasts, thighs, Marylands)
1 medium onion, peeled and finely chopped
125 g (4 oz) streaky bacon, rinds removed and chopped
125 g (4 oz) button mushrooms
½ cup hot chicken stock
2½ cups red wine
2 garlic cloves, peeled and crushed
30 g (1 oz) butter, cut into pieces
1 bouquet garni
1 tablespoon brandy (optional)
freshly ground black pepper
salt

Place the chicken pieces, skin downward, in a preheated browning dish, cover with a paper towel and cook for 8 minutes, turning once. Pour off fat and set aside.

Place the onion in a bowl, cover and cook on Maximum 2 minutes. Stir in bacon and cook uncovered 3 minutes, then mushrooms and cook 1 minute. Add to chicken with remaining ingredients except salt.

Cook covered on Maximum 6 minutes, then on Defrost 30 minutes. Halfway through, stir and season with salt. Before serving, remove the bouquet garni.

Clockwise: Chicken marengo; Coq au vin; Chicken liver and grapes; Chicken and peppers

SHERRY CHICKEN

Serves 4 Cooking time: 29 minutes
Microwave setting: Maximum (Full) and Medium High (¾ power)

- 4 chicken Marylands, total weight about 1.25 kg (2½ lb)
- 1 medium onion, peeled and sliced
- ¼ teaspoon chopped rosemary
- 2 teaspoons chopped parsley
- 1 teaspoon chopped tarragon
- 1 garlic clove, peeled and crushed
- 30 g (1 oz) butter, softened
- 2 tablespoons cornflour
- about 1¼ cups hot chicken stock
- ½ cup dry sherry
- ⅓ cup flaked almonds
- salt
- freshly ground black pepper
- 2 zucchini, sliced
- 2 tablespoons cream

Place the chicken skin side down in a preheated browning casserole. Cover with a paper towel and cook for 10 minutes, turning once. Set aside.

Place the onion, herbs and garlic in a bowl. Cover and cook for 5 minutes. Stir in the butter blended with cornflour. Make up the defatted chicken juices to 1¼ cups with the stock, then stir in with the sherry, almonds, zucchini and salt and pepper.

Cook uncovered for 4 minutes, stirring every minute. Stir in the cream.

Pour sauce over chicken. Cook, covered, 10 minutes.

TURKEY WITH ORANGE & ALMONDS

Serves 4 Cooking time: 8-10 minutes
Microwave setting: Maximum (Full)

- 4 skinless turkey fillets (schnitzels), total weight 400-500 g (14 oz-1 lb)
- freshly ground black pepper
- grated rind of 1 orange
- ⅓ cup flaked almonds, toasted
- 60 g (2 oz) butter
- ½ cup orange juice
- 1 tablespoon Grand Marnier
- 2 tablespoons brown sugar
- salt
- 1 orange, peeled and sliced, to garnish

Place the turkey in a shallow casserole and sprinkle with pepper. Cover and cook for 4-6 minutes, turning once. Set aside, covered.

Place the remaining ingredients except salt and sliced orange in a bowl. Cook uncovered for 2 minutes and season with salt and pepper.

Drain fillets, pour sauce over and cook, uncovered, for 2 minutes. Garnish with orange slices.

From left to right: Sherry chicken; Turkey with orange and almonds; Chicken in a bag; Turkey casserole

CHICKEN IN A BAG

Serves 4 Cooking time: 33½ minutes, plus standing
Microwave setting: Maximum (Full)

- 1 celery stick, finely chopped
- 1 medium onion, peeled and finely chopped
- 1 eating apple, peeled, cored and chopped
- 1 cup prunes, soaked in port overnight, stoned and chopped
- 1×No. 15 (1.5 kg/3 lb) roasting chicken
- 2 tablespoons honey
- 1 teaspoon Worcestershire sauce
- 1 teaspoon soy sauce
- parsley sprigs, to garnish

Place the celery, onion and apple in a bowl. Cover. Cook for 3½ minutes, then stir in prunes.

Spoon the stuffing into the chicken and truss it. Mix the honey, Worcestershire sauce and soy sauce together and brush over the chicken. Place the bird in a roasting bag, tie with string and prick the bag. Place the bird breast side down in a shallow dish.

Cook for 15 minutes. Turn over and cook for a further 15 minutes. Remove the chicken from the bag, tent loosely with foil and stand 15 minutes. Remove trussing string and garnish with parsley.

TURKEY CASSEROLE

Serves 4 Cooking time: 29 minutes
Microwave setting: Maximum (Full)

- 1.25 kg (2½ lb) turkey pieces, halved if large
- 1 celery stick, chopped
- 1 medium onion, peeled and chopped
- 1 carrot, peeled and sliced
- 1 tablespoon tomato paste
- 1 teaspoon chopped marjoram
- 1 teaspoon chopped thyme
- 1 tablespoon chopped parsley
- 30 g (1 oz) butter, cut into pieces
- 2 tablespoons plain flour
- about 1¾ cups chicken stock
- salt
- freshly ground black pepper
- chopped parsley, to garnish

Place the turkey pieces, skin side down, in a preheated browning casserole and cover with a paper towel. Cook uncovered for 12 minutes, turning over halfway through. Set aside, covered.

Place the vegetables, tomato paste and herbs in a large bowl. Cover and cook for 10 minutes, stirring halfway through cooking.

Stir in the butter until melted. Stir in the flour. Make up defatted turkey juices to 1¾ cups with stock, then stir in with salt and pepper. Cook uncovered for 3 minutes, stirring every minute.

Pour the vegetable sauce over the turkey. Cook uncovered for 4 minutes. Garnish with parsley.

CHICKEN IN SWEET & SOUR SAUCE

Serves 4 Cooking time: 28-29 minutes
Microwave setting: Maximum (Full)

4 chicken Marylands, total weight 1.25 kg (2½ lb), skinned
1 medium onion, peeled and chopped
½ green pepper, cored, seeded and diced
½ red pepper, cored, seeded and diced
1 garlic clove, peeled and crushed
30 g (1 oz) butter, diced
2 tablespoons plain flour
about 1¼ cups hot chicken stock
2 tablespoons white wine vinegar
1 tablespoon soy sauce
1 tablespoon marmalade
¾ cup dates, halved and stoned
⅓ cup brown sugar
freshly ground black pepper

Place chicken in a bowl, cover and cook for 10 minutes, rearranging once. Set aside, covered.

Place the onion, peppers and garlic in a bowl, cover and cook for 3-4 minutes, stirring halfway through. Stir in butter and cook for 2 minutes.

Stir in the flour and cook 1 minute. Make the chicken juices up to 1¼ cups with stock, then stir in with the remaining ingredients. Cover and cook for 3 minutes, stirring once. Add the chicken, cover and cook for 10 minutes.

CHAUDFROID CHICKEN

Serves 4 Cooking time: about 12½ minutes
Microwave setting: Maximum (Full)

1 piece of carrot
1 celery stick, halved
1 small onion, peeled
8 black peppercorns
1 bay leaf
2½ cups milk
2½ cups cold water
30 g (1 oz) aspic powder
60 g (2 oz) butter
4 tablespoons plain flour
1 teaspoon gelatine
2 tablespoons cream
salt
white pepper
4 chicken Marylands, total weight 1 kg (2 lb), cooked and skinned

To garnish:
4 long, thin strips of green pepper, to resemble flower stems
16 pieces of red pepper, cut into petal shapes
12 pieces of green pepper, cut into leaf shapes

Place the carrot, celery, onion, peppercorns, bay leaf and milk in a large jug. Cook uncovered for 4 minutes. Set aside for 15 minutes to infuse.

Meanwhile, place half of the cold water in a jug and cook uncovered for 3½ minutes. Stir in the aspic powder until dissolved, then stir in the remaining cold water. Stand the jug in a bowl of hot water.

Place the butter in a bowl and cook uncovered for 1 minute or until melted. Blend in the flour, then

gradually stir in the strained flavoured milk. Cook uncovered for 4 minutes, stirring every minute.

Stir the gelatine into ½ cup of the aspic mixture until dissolved. Beat this mixture into the sauce with the cream and salt and pepper to taste. Continue beating until smooth and glossy.

Place the chicken legs on a wire rack over a tray. Using a spoon, gently coat the chicken legs with the sauce. Continue coating the legs until completely covered.

Allow the sauce to set slightly before decorating, then arrange the pepper shapes on the chicken to represent flowers.

Using a spoon, slowly and gently coat the legs with 2 or 3 layers of the remaining aspic jelly. Chill until set.

Pour the remaining aspic jelly into a shallow tray and chill until set.

Using a knife, cut the jelly into small squares. Serve the chicken surrounded by diced jelly.

CHICKEN A LA KING

Serves 4 Cooking time: 12 minutes
Microwave setting: Maximum (Full)

125 g (4 oz) diced green pepper
125 g (4 oz) frozen peas
60 g (2 oz) butter, cut into small pieces
3 tablespoons plain flour
1¼ cups hot chicken stock
2 tablespoons dry sherry
500 g (1 lb) cooked chicken meat, diced
⅓ cup sour cream
salt
freshly ground black pepper

To garnish:
fried bread triangles (see page 15)
chopped parsley

Place the green pepper in a medium bowl, cover and cook for 1 minute. Stir in the peas, cover and cook for 3 minutes.

Stir in the butter until melted. Stir in the flour and cook 1 minute. Slowly blend in the stock and sherry and cook 4 minutes, stirring every minute. Stir in the chicken, sour cream, salt and pepper. Cook uncovered for 3 minutes, stirring once.

Arrange with bread triangles, garnish with parsley.

From left to right: Chicken in sweet and sour sauce; Chaudfroid chicken; Chicken a la king

TURKEY WITH MUSHROOMS

Serves 4 Cooking time: 16-18 minutes
Microwave setting: Maximum (Full)

4 skinless turkey fillets (schnitzels), total weight 400-500 g (14 oz-1 lb)
1 carrot, peeled and finely sliced
1 celery stick, finely sliced
1 medium onion, peeled and finely chopped
90 g (3 oz) button mushrooms, finely sliced
45 g (1½ oz) butter
3 tablespoons plain flour
¼ cup sherry
1¾ cups hot chicken stock
salt
freshly ground black pepper

Place the turkey in a large shallow casserole. Cover and cook for 4-6 minutes, turning once. Set aside.

Place the vegetables and butter in a medium bowl. Cover and cook for 4 minutes, stirring once. Stir in the flour and cook 1 minute. Stir in the sherry, stock, salt and pepper. Cover and cook for 3 minutes, stirring halfway through.

Pour over the turkey, cover and cook for 4 minutes.

CHICKEN WITH VERMOUTH

Serves 4 Cooking time: 26 minutes
Microwave setting: Maximum (Full)

1 medium onion, peeled and finely chopped
½ green pepper, cored, seeded and finely chopped
125 g (4 oz) mushrooms, sliced
1 teaspoon chopped basil
60 g (2 oz) butter
salt
freshly ground black pepper
4 chicken Marylands, total weight 1.25 kg (2½ lb), skinned
3 tablespoons cornflour
½ cup dry white vermouth
1¼ cups milk
1¼ cups hot chicken stock
flat-leaved parsley, to garnish

Place the onion and green pepper in a large bowl. Cover and cook for 4 minutes. Stir in the mushrooms, basil, butter, salt and pepper.

Arrange the chicken around the sides of the bowl, cover and cook for 8 minutes.

Stir the chicken and vegetables together and turn the bowl round. Cook for a further 7 minutes. Remove the chicken from the bowl and set aside.

Blend the cornflour and vermouth together, then stir

in the milk. Add to the vegetables. Stir in stock. Cool slightly, then puree in a blender.

Pour the sauce back into the bowl, cover and cook for 2 minutes.

Return the chicken to the bowl, cover and cook for 5 minutes. Garnish with parsley and serve.

GLAZED POUSSINS

Serves 4 Cooking time: 31 minutes, plus standing
Microwave setting: Maximum (Full)

30 g (1 oz) butter
1 tablespoon brown sugar
1 tablespoon Worcestershire sauce
4 bacon rashers, rinds removed
4×No. 4 (400 g/14 oz) chickens (poussins), trussed
watercress sprigs, to garnish

Place the butter, the sugar and Worcestershire sauce in a small bowl. Cook uncovered for 1 minute. Set aside.

Push a rasher of bacon into each chicken. Truss chickens and place on a roasting rack or upturned plates in a shallow dish. Cook uncovered 15 minutes, rearrange and brush with glaze, cook 15 minutes.

Tent chickens loosely with foil and stand 10 minutes. Remove string and garnish with watercress.

From left to right: Turkey with mushrooms; Chicken with vermouth; Glazed poussins

BRAISED PIGEONS

Serves 4 Cooking time: 26 minutes, plus standing
Microwave setting: Maximum (Full)

4 bacon rashers, rinds removed, then rolled
4 pigeons, total weight 1.25 kg (2½ lb)
2 small onions, peeled and sliced
60 g (2 oz) mushrooms, sliced
1 tablespoon tomato paste
1 teaspoon chopped thyme
1 teaspoon chopped parsley
¼ teaspoon chopped rosemary
½ teaspoon chopped marjoram
1 garlic clove, peeled and crushed
30 g (1 oz) butter, diced
2 tablespoons plain flour
1¼ cups hot chicken stock
1¼ cups red wine
salt
freshly ground black pepper

Place a bacon rasher inside each pigeon and truss the birds. Place breast side down in a shallow casserole. Cover and cook 5 minutes. Turn pigeons over and cook uncovered 5 minutes. Set aside, covered.

Place the onions, mushrooms, tomato paste, herbs and garlic in a medium bowl. Cover and cook for 5 minutes, stirring halfway through cooking.

Stir in butter until melted. Stir in flour, cook 1 minute and stir in the remaining ingredients. Cook uncovered for 5 minutes, stirring every minute.

Pour the sauce over the pigeons. Cover and cook for 6 minutes. Stand, covered, for 5 minutes.

ROAST PHEASANT WITH BREAD SAUCE

Serves 3-4 Cooking time: 27½ minutes, plus standing and grilling
Microwave setting: Maximum (Full)

1 medium onion, peeled
6 cloves
½ cup milk
½ cup cold chicken stock
2 cups fresh white breadcrumbs
90 g (3 oz) butter
salt
freshly ground black pepper
1×1 kg (2 lb) pheasant
3 streaky bacon rashers, rinds removed
1 tablespoon plain flour

To make the sauce, stud the onion with the cloves and place in a medium bowl. Add the milk, chicken stock, breadcrumbs, 60 g (2 oz) butter, salt and pepper. Cover, cook for 5½ minutes, stirring halfway.

Place the remaining butter inside the pheasant and secure the opening with trussing thread. Tie the bacon over the breast.

Place the pheasant in a roasting bag and tie with string. Prick the bag and place in a shallow casserole. Cook for 10 minutes. Turn the pheasant over and cook for a further 10 minutes.

Remove the pheasant from the bag and discard the bacon. Wrap in foil. Stand for 10 minutes.

Place the pheasant in a grill pan. Sprinkle with flour and **brown under a preheated conventional grill.**

Meanwhile, remove and discard the onion from the sauce. Cook for 2 minutes, stirring halfway.

RABBIT IN WHITE WINE

Serves 4 Cooking time: 29 minutes, plus standing
Microwave setting: Maximum (Full) and Medium (½ power)

1 medium onion, peeled and finely chopped
1 celery stick, finely sliced
1 carrot, peeled and finely diced
½ green pepper, cored, seeded and finely diced
1 garlic clove, peeled and crushed
½ teaspoon chopped rosemary
1 teaspoon chopped parsley
60 g (2 oz) butter
8 rabbit joints, total weight 750 g-1 kg (1½-2 lb)
2½ tablespoons cornflour
½ cup milk
1¼ cups hot chicken stock
½ cup white wine
salt
freshly ground black pepper
rosemary sprigs, to garnish

Place the vegetables, herbs and butter in a large bowl. Cover and cook 4 minutes on Maximum, stirring halfway through cooking.

Place the rabbit round the sides of the bowl. Cover and cook 5 minutes. Stir rabbit and vegetables together and turn the bowl round. Cook on Medium 16 minutes. Remove rabbit. Stir in cornflour blended with milk, then stock, wine, salt and pepper.

Return the rabbit to the bowl, cover and cook for 4 minutes. Stand, covered, 10 minutes before serving garnished with rosemary.

DUCK WITH RED WINE SAUCE

Serves 4 Cooking time: 36 minutes, plus grilling
Microwave setting: Maximum (Full)

1×No. 20 (2 kg/4½ lb) duck, quartered
3 tomatoes, skinned and chopped
1 medium onion, peeled and finely chopped
60 g (2 oz) butter
1 tablespoon tomato paste
2 garlic cloves, peeled and crushed
½ teaspoon chopped rosemary
1 teaspoon chopped basil
salt
freshly ground black pepper
3 tablespoons cornflour
½ cup dry red wine
1¾ cups hot chicken stock

Prick the duck skin and place the pieces on a roasting rack or upturned plate in a large shallow dish. Cook, covered, for 25 minutes, turning the dish round once.

Place the duck in a grill pan and **brown under a preheated conventional grill.** Keep hot.

Place the tomatoes, onion, butter, tomato paste, garlic, herbs, salt and pepper in a large bowl. Cover and cook for 8 minutes. Stir in the cornflour blended with wine, then the stock. Cool slightly, then puree in a blender.

Return to the bowl and cook for 3 minutes or until thickened and hot, stirring halfway through.

Serve duck with sauce.

Clockwise: Rabbit in white wine; Duck with red wine sauce; Roast pheasant with bread sauce; Braised pigeons

ROAST DUCK

Serves 4-6 Cooking time: 40 minutes, plus standing and grilling
Microwave setting: Maximum (Full)

1×No. 22 (2.2 kg/5 lb) duck, washed and cleaned
1 orange, cut into 8 pieces

Stuff the duck with the orange pieces. Prick the skin and truss. Place in a roasting bag, tie with string and pierce the bag. Place the bird, breast side down, on a roasting rack or upturned plate in a shallow dish. Cook for 20 minutes.

Drain off juices, remove duck from bag and cook uncovered, breast side up, for 20 minutes. Tent loosely with foil and stand 15 minutes. **Brown under a preheated conventional grill, in portions if necessary.**

SPICED DUCK

Serves 4 Cooking time: 30½-35½ minutes, plus standing and grilling
Microwave setting: Maximum (Full)

1×No. 20 (2 kg/4 lb) duck
1 large onion, peeled and chopped
3 tablespoons brown sugar
1½ teaspoons salt
2 tablespoons paprika
2 tablespoons tomato paste
2 tablespoons Worcestershire sauce
4 tablespoons white wine vinegar
4 tablespoons lemon juice
½ teaspoon chopped rosemary
2 teaspoons snipped chives
½ teaspoon grated nutmeg
3½ cups cold water
freshly ground black pepper
30 g (1 oz) butter
2 tablespoons plain flour
green shallot brushes, to garnish

Plunge the duck into boiling water for 5 minutes, drain and cut into quarters. Prick the skin all over.

Place the onion, sugar, salt, paprika, tomato paste, Worcestershire sauce, vinegar, lemon juice, herbs, nutmeg, water and pepper in a large bowl. Add the duck and leave overnight.

Drain, reserving the marinade. Place on a roasting rack or upturned plate in a shallow dish, cover and cook for 20-25 minutes, pouring off juice and rearranging pieces after 10 minutes. Leave to stand, covered, 10 minutes, then place the duck on a grill pan and **grill under a preheated conventional grill** until the skin is crisp.

Meantime, place the butter in a large bowl and cook uncovered for 30 seconds or until melted. Stir in the flour, cook 1 minute. Stir in 2½ cups of the strained, reserved marinade and cook uncovered for 5 minutes, stirring every minute.

Serve the duck with the sauce, garnished with shallots.

Roast duck; Spiced duck

STUFFED ROAST TURKEY

Serves 7-8 Cooking time: 50 minutes, plus standing
Microwave setting: Maximum (Full)

30 g (1 oz) butter
1 large onion, peeled and finely chopped
1 cup fresh white breadcrumbs
1 cup fresh brown breadcrumbs
½ cup hot chicken stock
1 teaspoon chopped thyme
¼ teaspoon chopped rosemary
1 teaspoon chopped marjoram
1 tablespoon chopped parsley
¼ teaspoon chopped sage
1 orange, peeled and chopped
grated rind of 1 orange
2 tablespoons sultanas
salt
freshly ground black pepper
1×No. 30 (3 kg/7 lb) turkey, thawed if frozen and at room temperature
watercress, to garnish

Glaze:
60 g (2 oz) butter
2 tablespoons brown sugar
2 teaspoons sherry
2 teaspoons soy sauce

If using a different size turkey, allow 7½ minutes per 500 g (1 lb) for turkeys under No. 45 (4.5 kg/7 lb). Place the butter and onion in a medium bowl, cover and cook for 2 minutes. Stir in the remaining ingredients except for glaze. Stuff and truss the turkey.

Mask the wings and legs with pieces of foil. Place the turkey, breast side down, on an inverted plate or roasting rack in a shallow dish. Cover with a paper towel. Cook for 25 minutes. Set aside.

Place glaze ingredients in a small jug, cook 1½ minutes.

Remove foil from turkey, turn over and brush with glaze. Cook 25 minutes, then tent loosely with foil and stand for 30 minutes. Garnish with watercress and serve with sauces, gravy and vegetables.

CHRISTMAS LUNCH

Honeyed Grapefruit and Orange

Roast Turkey
Cranberry Relish
Peas
Potatoes, or roast potatoes
Gravy
Bread Sauce

Christmas Pudding

Order of cooking:
Earlier in the day, prepare the starter ingredients (page 26), stuff the turkey, prepare the potatoes (page 105), make the cranberry and bread sauces (page 140), and mix the Christmas Pudding (page 121).

Cook the turkey and, while standing, cook the potatoes. During the potato standing time, cook the peas, make the gravy and reheat the bread sauce for about 3 minutes.

Cook the pudding while serving the main course.

Honeyed grapefruit and orange; Christmas pudding; Bread sauce; Peas; Roast Turkey; Potatoes; Gravy; Cranberry Relish

Fish pie; Fish risotto

FISH

FISH PIE

Serves 4 Cooking time: 23½ minutes
Microwave setting: Maximum (Full)

500 g (1 lb) smoked haddock fillets
3 tablespoons water
salt
750 g (1½ lb) potatoes, peeled and cubed
about 4 tablespoons milk
15 g (½ oz) butter
freshly ground black pepper

Sauce:
30 g (1 oz) butter
2 tablespoons plain flour
salt
freshly ground black pepper
1 hard-boiled egg, finely chopped
parsley sprigs, to garnish

Place the fish in a large bowl. Cover and cook for 5 minutes, rearranging halfway through cooking. Set aside, covered.

Place the water, salt and potatoes in a large bowl. Cover and cook for 10 minutes. Set aside, covered.

Drain the liquid from the fish and make up to 1¼ cups with milk.

To make the sauce, place the butter in a large bowl and cook for 30 seconds. Stir in the flour and cook 1 minute. Stir in the milk and salt and pepper to taste. Cook for 4 minutes, stirring every minute.

Flake the fish, removing any skin and bones. Fold into the sauce with the chopped egg.

Mash the potatoes with the butter, remaining milk and pepper to taste.

Pour the fish mixture into a shallow casserole. Pipe the potatoes over the fish. Cook uncovered 4 minutes. Garnish with sprigs of parsley and serve with peas.

FISH RISOTTO

Serves 4-6 Cooking time: 29 minutes, plus standing
Microwave setting: Maximum (Full)

60 g (2 oz) butter
1 large onion, peeled and finely chopped
½ green pepper, cored, seeded and finely diced
½ red pepper, cored, seeded and finely diced
1 tablespoon tomato paste
1 garlic clove, peeled and crushed
1 tablespoon chopped parsley
60 g (2 oz) mushrooms, finely chopped
1½ cups long-grain rice
2½ cups hot chicken stock
salt
¼ teaspoon oil
750 g (1½ lb) fish fillets, rinsed in cold water
¼ cup grated cheese
freshly ground black pepper

Place the butter, onion, peppers, tomato paste, garlic, parsley and mushrooms in a large bowl. Cover and cook for 6 minutes, stirring halfway through.

Stir in the rice, stock, salt and oil. Cover and cook for 12 minutes. Stir halfway through cooking. Set aside, covered.

Place the fillets in a shallow dish. Cover and cook for 7 minutes, rearranging halfway through cooking. Leave to stand for 4 minutes, covered.

Flake the fish, removing skin. Fold the fish and cheese into the rice mixture and season with pepper.

STEAMED FISH

Serves 4 Cooking time: 6 minutes, plus standing
Microwave setting: Maximum (Full)

500 g (1 lb) fish fillets (e.g. gemfish, redfish, bream)

To garnish:
lemon slices
parsley sprigs

The addition of water is unnecessary in this recipe.

Place the fish in a shallow dish. Cover and cook for 6 minutes.

Leave to stand, covered, for 3-4 minutes or until the fish is opaque and the flesh flakes slightly when tested with a fork. Serve garnished with lemon slices and parsley sprigs.

From left to right: Steamed fish; Herb-stuffed fish steaks; Stuffed trout; Mullet roll-ups

HERB-STUFFED FISH STEAKS

Serves 4 Cooking time: 9 minutes, plus standing
Microwave setting: Maximum (Full)

1 small onion, peeled and chopped
2 teaspoons chopped thyme
2 teaspoons chopped parsley
¼ teaspoon chopped rosemary
¼ teaspoon chopped sage
1 cup fresh white breadcrumbs
3 tablespoons water
salt
freshly ground black pepper
4 fish steaks, total weight 750 g (1½ lb)
30 g (1 oz) butter, cut into pieces

Place the onion in a medium bowl, cover and cook for 2 minutes. Stir in the thyme, parsley, rosemary, sage, breadcrumbs, water and salt and pepper to taste. Set aside.

Place the fish steaks, thin ends to the centre, in a shallow casserole. Cover and cook for 4 minutes.

Remove bones and stuff each steak with the herb mixture. Sprinkle with pepper and dot with the butter. Cover and cook for 3 minutes. Leave to stand, covered, for 3 minutes before serving.

Serve with noodles and Cauliflower Cheese (page 102).

STUFFED TROUT

Serves 4 Cooking time: 12 minutes, plus standing
Microwave setting: Maximum (Full)

¼ cup flaked almonds
125 g (4 oz) small cooked, peeled prawns
4 tablespoons fresh white breadcrumbs
2 tablespoons lemon juice
salt
freshly ground black pepper
4 trout, about 250 g (8 oz) each, cleaned, with heads left on

To garnish:
parsley sprigs
lemon slices

Mix together the almonds, prawns, breadcrumbs, lemon juice and plenty of salt and pepper to taste.
Fill trout with the stuffing. Cover and cook for 12 minutes, rearranging once. Leave to stand, covered, for 3 minutes. Garnish with parsley and lemon.

MULLET ROLL-UPS

Serves 4 Cooking time: 6-7 minutes, plus standing
Microwave setting: Maximum (Full)

1½ cups fresh brown breadcrumbs
1 teaspoon chopped marjoram
1 teaspoon chopped thyme
2 teaspoons chopped parsley
½ teaspoon chopped sage
grated rind of 1 lemon
2 tablespoons lemon juice
1 teaspoon anchovy sauce
6 tablespoons hot water
salt
freshly ground black pepper
750 g (1½ lb) mullet fillets

To garnish:
lemon slices
parsley sprigs

Mix together the breadcrumbs, marjoram, thyme, parsley, sage, lemon rind, lemon juice, anchovy sauce, water, and salt and pepper to taste.
Spread the stuffing over the fish. Roll up from the head end to the tail. Secure with toothpicks. Cover and cook for 5-6 minutes, rearranging halfway through cooking.
Leave to stand, covered, for 5 minutes before serving, garnished with lemon slices and parsley.

FISH WITH MUSTARD SAUCE

Serves 4 Cooking time: 12-16 minutes
Microwave setting: Maximum (Full)

1 small onion, peeled and chopped
1 teaspoon chopped thyme
1 teaspoon chopped marjoram
grated rind of ½ lemon
1 cup fresh brown breadcrumbs
salt
freshly ground black pepper
1 egg
4 small whole fish, total weight 750 g (1½ lb), scaled and cleaned

Sauce:
45 g (1½ oz) butter
2 tablespoons plain flour
1¾ cups milk
1 tablespoon dry mustard
1 tablespoon white wine vinegar
1 teaspoon caster sugar
salt
freshly ground black pepper
chopped parsley, to garnish

Place the onion in a small bowl, cover and cook for 2 minutes. Stir in the herbs, lemon rind, breadcrumbs, salt, pepper and egg.

Fill the fish with the stuffing. Close and secure with wooden toothpicks. Place the fish in a shallow casserole, cover and cook for 4-6 minutes, turning over after 2 minutes. Set aside, covered, while making the sauce.

Place the butter in a large bowl and cook for 1 minute or until melted. Stir in the flour and cook 1 minute. Gradually blend in the milk, mustard, vinegar, sugar and salt and pepper to taste. Cook for 4-6 minutes until thickened, stirring every minute. Remove toothpicks from the fish and pour sauce over. Sprinkle with chopped parsley and serve with new potatoes.

CHEESY SMOKED HADDOCK

Serves 4 Cooking time: 12-13 minutes
Microwave setting: Maximum (Full)

600 g (1¼ lb) smoked haddock fillets
30 g (1 oz) butter, softened

Cheese sauce:
30 g (1 oz) butter
2 tablespoons plain flour
1¼ cups milk
1 teaspoon prepared mustard
salt
freshly ground black pepper
½ cup grated Cheddar cheese
flat-leaved parsley, to garnish

Spread the haddock fillets with butter and place in a plastic bag, tie with string and prick the bag. Cook for 5 minutes. Set aside.

Place the butter in a large bowl and cook for 1 minute or until melted. Blend in the flour and cook 1 minute. Stir in the milk, mustard and salt and pepper. Cook uncovered for 4-5 minutes, stirring every minute.

Stir in the cheese and cook uncovered for 1 minute.

Drain the fish and arrange on a serving dish. Pour over the sauce. Garnish with sprigs of parsley.

BAKED FISH STEAKS WITH CAPERS

Serves 4 Cooking time: 16 minutes
Microwave setting: Maximum (Full)

30 g (1 oz) butter
4 fish steaks, total weight 750 g (1½ lb)

Sauce:
30 g (1 oz) butter
1½ tablespoons cornflour
1¼ cups milk
salt
freshly ground black pepper
2 tablespoons capers, drained and chopped
1 tablespoon caper juice
dill sprigs, to garnish

Place the butter in a small dish. Cook for 1 minute or until melted.

Brush the fish steaks with the butter. Arrange the fish in a shallow casserole, cover and cook for 8 minutes, turning once. Set aside, covered.

To make the sauce, place the butter in a bowl. Cook for 1 minute or until melted. Stir in the cornflour blended with the milk, and salt and pepper. Cook for 4 minutes, stirring every minute.

Stir in the capers and their juice and pour the sauce over the fish. Cook for 2 minutes. Garnish with dill.

FILLETS OF FISH VERONIQUE

Serves 4 Cooking time: 19-20 minutes
Microwave setting: Maximum (Full)

60 g (2 oz) button mushrooms, finely diced
1 medium onion, peeled and finely chopped
125 g (4 oz) butter
1¼ cups dry white wine
1 kg (2 lb) skinned fillets of white fish
4 tablespoons plain flour
1¼ cups milk
salt
freshly ground black pepper
125 g (4 oz) white grapes, peeled, halved and seeded
lemon slices, to garnish

Place the mushrooms, onion, half the butter and wine in a shallow casserole. Cover and cook for 4 minutes. Roll up the fish fillets, skinned side inward, and place in the casserole. Cover and cook 7-8 minutes, turning over once. Drain, reserving liquid, and keep hot.

Place remaining butter in a large bowl. Cook for 1 minute or until melted. Blend in the flour, cook 1 minute, then stir in the fish liquid, milk, salt and pepper. Cook for 5 minutes, stirring every minute.

Stir in the grapes. Pour the sauce over the fish, cover and cook for 1 minute. Garnish with lemon.

Clockwise: Fish with mustard sauce; Baked fish steaks with capers; Fillets of fish veronique; Cheesy smoked haddock

FISH STEAKS GARNI

Serves 4 Cooking time: 7 minutes
Microwave setting: Maximum (Full)

4 fish steaks, total weight 750 g (1½ lb)
salt
freshly ground black pepper
30 g (1 oz) butter, cut into 4 pieces
1×50 g can anchovy fillets, drained
16 capers

To garnish:
lemon slices
parsley sprigs

Place the fish steaks, with the thin ends to the centre, in a dish. Cover and cook for 4 minutes.

Season the steaks with salt and pepper and turn over. Place a piece of butter on each. Cover and cook for 1½ minutes.

Baste the fish with the melted butter. Arrange a cross of 2 anchovies on each steak with capers in between. Cook uncovered for 1½ minutes. Garnish with lemon slices and parsley.

FISH FILLETS WITH SWEETCORN

Serves 4 Cooking time: about 8½ minutes
Microwave setting: Maximum (Full)

600 g (1¼ lb) small, skinned fish fillets
90 g (3 oz) butter, cut into pieces
1×310 g can cream-style sweetcorn
1 slice onion
salt
freshly ground black pepper
parsley sprigs, to garnish

Roll up the fillets and place in a shallow casserole. Cover and cook for 3½ minutes. Set aside, covered.

Place the butter in a jug and cook uncovered for 1 minute or until melted.

Place the butter, sweetcorn and onion in a blender. Blend until smooth and season with salt and pepper.

Rearrange the fillets. Sprinkle with salt and pepper to taste, and spoon sweetcorn mixture over the top.

Cook uncovered for 4 minutes.

Garnish with sprigs of parsley and serve immediately.

From left to right: Fish steaks garni; Fish fillets with sweetcorn; Sole and prawn rolls; Spiced gemfish

SOLE & PRAWN ROLLS

Serves 4-6 Cooking time: 6-7 minutes
Microwave setting: Maximum (Full)

750 g (1½ lb) skinned sole or flounder fillets
lemon juice
185 g (6 oz) shelled weight prawns, chopped
3 tablespoons chopped parsley
salt
freshly ground black pepper
60 g (2 oz) butter, cut into pieces
chopped parsley, to garnish

Cut the fillets lengthwise in half if large. Sprinkle the prawns with lemon juice, then spread over the fillets (skinned side). Sprinkle over the parsley, salt and pepper.

Roll up and secure with toothpicks.

Place in a shallow casserole, cover and cook for 4 minutes. Rearrange, dot with butter, cover and cook for 2-3 minutes.

Remove toothpicks. Garnish with chopped parsley and serve with duchesse potatoes and fried zucchini or green beans.

SPICED GEMFISH

Serves 4 Cooking time: 9-9½ minutes
Microwave setting: Maximum (Full)

30 g (1 oz) ghee
1 small onion, peeled and chopped
750 g (1½ lb) skinned gemfish fillets, cut into pieces
60 g (2 oz) button mushrooms, sliced
1 garlic clove, peeled and crushed
2 tablespoons Worcestershire sauce
1 tablespoon chopped, mixed herbs
½ teaspoon curry powder
1 teaspoon soy sauce
1×410 g can tomatoes, chopped with their juice
salt
freshly ground black pepper

Place the ghee and onion in a large bowl, cover and cook for 2 minutes.

Stir in the fish, mushrooms, garlic, Worcestershire sauce, herbs, curry powder and soy sauce. Cover and cook for 3½-4 minutes, stirring halfway through cooking.

Stir in the tomatoes and salt and pepper to taste. Cook uncovered for 3½ minutes.

Serve surrounded by boiled rice with peas.

SNAPPER STEAKS WITH CARROT & ONION TOPPING

Serves 4 Cooking time: about 17 minutes
Microwave setting: Maximum (Full)

1 medium onion, peeled and finely chopped
250 g (8 oz) carrots, peeled and finely grated
4 snapper steaks, total weight 750 g (1½ lb)
60 g (2 oz) butter
salt
freshly ground black pepper
parsley sprigs, to garnish

Place the onion in a medium bowl, cover and cook for 2 minutes. Stir in the carrots, cover and cook for 5 minutes. Set aside, covered.

Place the snapper steaks, with the thin ends to the centre, in a shallow casserole dish, cover and cook for 6 minutes. Set aside.

Place the butter in a small jug and cook uncovered for 1 minute or until melted. Stir the butter into the vegetables and season to taste with salt and pepper. Stir in the liquid from the fish.

Top the fish steaks with the carrot mixture and pour over any juice. Cook uncovered for 3 minutes.

Garnish with the parsley sprigs.

LEMON TROUT

Serves 4 Cooking time: 8 minutes, plus standing
Microwave setting: Maximum (Full)

1 lemon, cut into 8 wedges
4 trout, about 185 g (6 oz) each, cleaned, with heads left on
grated rind of 2 lemons
60 g (2 oz) butter, cut into 8 pieces

To garnish:
4 lemon twists
parsley sprigs

Place 2 wedges of lemon inside each trout. Place in a shallow casserole dish. Cover and cook for 3 minutes.

Turn the trout over. Sprinkle with the lemon rind and dot with the butter. Cover and cook for 5 minutes, basting with butter after 1 minute.

Leave to stand, covered, for 3 minutes. Garnish with lemon twists and parsley, and serve with a fresh green salad.

Snapper steaks with carrot and onion topping; Lemon trout; Fish in savoury sauce; Fish in a bag

FISH IN SAVOURY SAUCE

Serves 4 Cooking time: 10-14 minutes
Microwave setting: Maximum (Full)

1 medium onion, peeled and finely sliced
4 tomatoes, skinned and chopped
1 tablespoon tomato paste
1 teaspoon chopped thyme
2 teaspoons chopped parsley
1 teaspoon chopped marjoram
¼ teaspoon chopped rosemary
1 garlic clove, peeled and crushed
30 g (1 oz) butter
salt
freshly ground black pepper
4 fish steaks, total weight 750 g (1½ lb)
fresh dill, to garnish

Place the onion, tomatoes, tomato paste, herbs, garlic, butter, salt and pepper in a large bowl. Cover and cook 4-6 minutes, stirring once. Set aside, covered, while cooking the fish.

Place the fish in a shallow dish. Cover and cook for 3 minutes. Turn fish over and cook a further 1-3 minutes.

Pour the sauce over the fish, cover and cook for 2 minutes, then garnish with dill.

FISH IN A BAG

Serves 4 Cooking time: 12 minutes, plus standing
Microwave setting: Maximum (Full)

60 g (2 oz) butter
4 whole fish, total weight 1.5 kg (3 lb), cleaned
1 tablespoon chopped parsley
salt
freshly ground black pepper
lemon wedges and parsley sprigs, to garnish

Spread the butter inside each of the fish. Sprinkle the parsley over the butter in the fish and season with salt and pepper. If the fish are too big to fit inside the oven, remove the heads. Place each fish in a freezer bag, tie with string and prick bags.

Place the fish side by side on a large plate. Cook for 4 minutes.

Turn the fish over and cook for a further 4 minutes. Turn again and cook for 4 minutes longer.

Leave to stand in the bags for 4 minutes. Serve garnished with lemon wedges and parsley.

TUNA MOUSSE

Serves 4 Cooking time: 6 minutes
Microwave setting: Maximum (Full)

30 g (1 oz) butter
2 tablespoons plain flour
1¼ cups cold chicken stock
¼ teaspoon ground mace
5 teaspoons gelatine
4 tablespoons dry sherry
1¼ cups mayonnaise
2 teaspoons anchovy sauce
2×200 g cans tuna, drained and flaked
salt
freshly ground black pepper
½ cup cream, whipped

To garnish:
slices of lemon
parsley sprigs

Place the butter in a bowl and cook for 1 minute or until melted.

Blend in the flour and cook 1 minute. Stir in the stock and mace and cook a further 3½ minutes, stirring 2 or 3 times. Set aside.

Place the gelatine in a small bowl and stir in the sherry. Cook for 30 seconds until dissolved. Stir to dissolve completely.

Whisk the sherry gelatine liquid into the sauce. Set aside to cool slightly.

Stir the mayonnaise, anchovy sauce, tuna, salt and pepper into the sauce. Fold in the cream.

Gently pour the mixture into a wetted 5-cup mould. Chill for at least 4 hours or until set.

Turn out and garnish with lemon and parsley.

GEMFISH MOUSSE

Serves 4-6 Cooking time: 5½-6½ minutes
Microwave setting: Maximum (Full)

500 g (1 lb) gemfish fillets, cut into pieces
30 g (1 oz) aspic powder
1¼ cups hot water
1 tablespoon chopped parsley
salt
freshly ground black pepper
3 tablespoons sour cream
2 egg whites

To garnish:
cucumber slices
watercress sprigs

Place the fillets in a bowl, cover and cook 5-6 minutes, rearranging halfway. Set aside, covered.

Stir the aspic powder into the hot water. Cook uncovered for 30 seconds. Stir well to dissolve.

Drain and skin the fish and puree in a food processor. Mix with the aspic, parsley, salt and pepper to taste. Cool completely, stir in the sour cream.

Whisk the egg whites until stiff. Gently fold into the fish mixture, spoon into a wetted 3-cup ring mould and chill until set. Turn out and serve garnished with cucumber and watercress.

Left: Tuna mousse; Gemfish mousse. Right: Poached trout; Fruit salad; Vichyssoise; Mixed green salad and potato salad

DINNER PARTY

Vichyssoise

Poached Trout
Mixed Green Salad
Potato Salad

Fruit Salad

Order of cooking:
Prepare and cook Vichyssoise (page 21), Trout, Potato Salad (page 111) and Fruit Salad (page 126) earlier in the day.
Prepare the mixed salad ingredients.

POACHED TROUT

Serves 4 Cooking time: 12 minutes, plus standing
Microwave setting: Maximum (Full)

1 or 2 large trout, total weight 1.5 kg (3 lb)
mayonnaise, to serve

Remove eyes from trout. Cover a large plate with plastic film and place the fish on it. Cook covered for 12 minutes, turning plate halfway through. Leave, covered, for 5 minutes. Remove cover and cool. Remove skin from upper side of fish.
Garnish with piped mayonnaise.

BUTTERED JERUSALEM ARTICHOKES

Serves 4 Cooking time: 9 minutes, plus standing
Microwave setting: Maximum (Full)

3 tablespoons water
2 teaspoons lemon juice
500 g (1 lb) Jerusalem artichokes, peeled and sliced
salt
45 g (1½ oz) butter, cut into pieces
1 tablespoon chopped parsley, to garnish

Place the water, lemon juice, salt and artichokes in a large bowl. Cover and cook for 9 minutes, stirring and adding salt halfway through cooking.

Leave to stand, covered, for 5 minutes.

Drain and toss in the butter. Garnish with parsley.

CROQUETTE POTATOES

Serves 4 Cooking time: 11½-13 minutes
Microwave setting: Maximum (Full)

3 tablespoons water
750 g (1½ lb) potatoes, peeled and chopped
30 g (1 oz) butter
1½ teaspoons milk
salt
freshly ground black pepper
1 egg, lightly beaten
1 cup toasted breadcrumbs

Place the water in a large bowl. Add the potatoes, cover and cook for 9 minutes. Leave to stand, covered, for 5 minutes.

Beat the butter, milk and salt and pepper to taste into the potatoes. Roll the mixture into 16 cork shapes. Chill for 30 minutes for a firmer texture.

Coat the croquettes with egg and roll in breadcrumbs. Place on a piece of paper towel, in a circle. Prick with a fork. Cook uncovered for 2½-4 minutes, turning over halfway through cooking.

CAULIFLOWER CHEESE

Serves 4-6 Cooking time: about 18 minutes
Microwave setting: Maximum (Full)

1 cauliflower, prepared weight 750 g (1½ lb)

Sauce:
30 g (1 oz) butter
2 tablespoons plain flour
1¼ cups milk
salt
freshly ground black pepper
1 teaspoon made English mustard
½ cup grated Cheddar cheese
chopped parsley, to garnish

Rinse the cauliflower in water and place it in a medium bowl. Cover and cook for 10 minutes, turning the cauliflower over halfway through cooking. Keep hot while making the sauce.

Place the butter in a bowl. Cook for 1 minute or until melted.

Blend in the flour and cook 1 minute. Stir in the milk, salt, pepper and mustard. Cook for 5 minutes, stirring every minute.

Stir in the cheese and cook for 1 minute.

Pour the sauce over the cauliflower and garnish with the parsley.

From left to right: Buttered Jerusalem artichokes; Croquette potatoes; Cauliflower cheese

VEGETABLES

CABBAGE WITH CARAWAY

Serves 4-6 Cooking time: 8 minutes
Microwave setting: Maximum (Full)

3 tablespoons water
375 g (12 oz) cabbage, stalk removed and finely shredded
1 tablespoon caraway seeds
salt
15 g (½ oz) butter

Place the water in a large bowl. Place the cabbage on top. Cover and cook for 8 minutes. Halfway through cooking, stir in the caraway seeds and salt.

Stir the butter into the cabbage until melted.

BOILED POTATOES

Serves 4 Cooking time: 9 minutes, plus standing
Microwave setting: Maximum (Full)

3 tablespoons cold water
750 g (1½ lb) potatoes, peeled and cut in half
30 g (1 oz) butter, cut into pieces
1 tablespoon chopped parsley
salt

Place the water in a large bowl. Add the potatoes, cover and cook for 9 minutes, stirring halfway through. Stand, covered for 8-10 minutes.

Drain off the water. Add the butter and parsley and toss to coat the potatoes. Season with salt if desired.

PARSNIPS WITH PARSLEY

Serves 4-6 Cooking time: 8 minutes, plus standing
Microwave setting: Maximum (Full)

3 tablespoons water
1 tablespoon chopped parsley
750 g (1½ lb) parsnips, peeled and quartered
15 g (½ oz) butter
salt

Place the water and parsley in a large bowl. Add the parsnips. Cover and cook for 8 minutes, stirring halfway through.

Stand, covered, for 5 minutes. Strain, then stir in the butter until melted. Season with salt if desired.

MINTED PEAS

Serves 4-6 Cooking time: 4-6 minutes
Microwave setting: Maximum (Full)

3 tablespoons water
1 teaspoon chopped mint
500 g (1 lb) frozen peas
30 g (1 oz) butter, diced
salt

Place the water, mint and peas in a medium bowl. Cover and cook for 4-6 minutes, stirring halfway through cooking. Drain.

Toss in butter. Season with salt if desired.

Clockwise: Braised celery; Sweetcorn; Minted peas; Parsnips with parsley; Green beans; Vichy carrots; Boiled potatoes; Cabbage with caraway

BRAISED CELERY

Serves 4-6 Cooking time: 10 minutes, plus standing
Microwave setting: Maximum (Full)

3 tablespoons water
500 g (1 lb) celery, trimmed and cut into short lengths
1 medium onion, peeled and thinly sliced
½ cup hot chicken stock
30 g (1 oz) butter, cut into pieces
1 teaspoon chopped parsley
salt
freshly ground black pepper

Place the water in an oblong casserole dish. Place half the celery in the dish and spread over the onion. Cover the onion with the remaining celery. Cover and cook for 8 minutes. After 4 minutes of cooking, rearrange the vegetables.

Mix together the hot stock, butter, parsley, and salt and pepper to taste. Pour over the celery, cover and cook for 2 minutes. Leave to stand, covered, for 3-4 minutes before serving.

VICHY CARROTS

Serves 4 Cooking time: 6-9 minutes
Microwave setting: Maximum (Full)

3 tablespoons cold water
1 teaspoon caster sugar
500 g (1 lb) carrots, peeled and thinly sliced
30 g (1 oz) butter, cut into pieces
1 tablespoon chopped parsley

Place the water, sugar and carrots in a medium bowl. Cover and cook for 6-9 minutes or until tender, stirring halfway through cooking.

Drain and stir in the butter until melted. Fold in the parsley. Serve hot. If serving with the Guard of Honour (page 63), stand covered until the corn has heated and then drain and complete the recipe.

GREEN BEANS

Serves 4 Cooking time: 8 minutes, plus standing
Microwave setting: Maximum (Full)

500 g (1 lb) whole green beans
salt

Place the beans in a medium bowl (no added water is needed). Cover and cook for 8 minutes, stirring halfway through cooking. Leave to stand, covered, for 2 minutes.

Drain, sprinkle with salt if desired and toss before serving.

SWEETCORN

Serves 4 Cooking time: 6 minutes
Microwave setting: Maximum (Full)

1½ cups freshly cut sweetcorn kernels
freshly ground black pepper
30 g (1 oz) butter, cut into pieces

Place the sweetcorn in a dish, cover and cook for 6 minutes, stirring halfway through. Season with pepper and stir in butter until melted.

CABBAGE PARCELS

Serves 4 Cooking time: 16-18 minutes, plus standing
Microwave setting: Maximum (Full)

8 cabbage leaves, trimmed of heavy stems
1 medium onion, peeled and finely chopped
250 g (8 oz) tomatoes, skinned and chopped
15 g (½ oz) butter, softened
2 tablespoons plain flour
1¼ cups hot beef stock
½ teaspoon Worcestershire sauce
2 teaspoons chopped, mixed herbs
salt
freshly ground black pepper
4 tablespoons cooked rice

Place the cabbage leaves in a plastic bag, tie with string and prick the bag. Cook 2-4 minutes or until soft and wilted. Drain.

Place the onion and tomatoes in a medium bowl. Cover and cook for 4 minutes. Stir in the butter blended with the flour, cook 1 minute. Stir in the remaining ingredients. Cook uncovered for 2 minutes.

Place a little of the mixture on each of the cabbage leaves. Fold the leaves over to make parcels.

Arrange the cabbage parcels, seam sides down, in a shallow dish, cover and cook for 7 minutes, turning the dish round halfway through cooking. Leave to stand, covered, for 5 minutes.

BROCCOLI WITH CHEESE SAUCE

Serves 4-6 Cooking time: 11-13 minutes
Microwave setting: Maximum (Full)

500 g (1 lb) fresh broccoli, stalks halved lengthwise

Sauce:
30 g (1 oz) butter
2 tablespoons plain flour
1¼ cups milk
1 teaspoon made English mustard
salt
freshly ground black pepper
½ cup grated Cheddar cheese

Arrange the broccoli on a plate, in a circle with the stems to the outside. Cover with plastic film and cook 6-8 minutes until tender. Set aside, covered.

Place the butter in a bowl. Cook for 1 minute or until melted. Blend in the flour, cook 1 minute, then stir in the milk, mustard and salt and pepper to taste. Cook for 3 minutes, stirring every minute. Stir in the cheese. Cook for 1 minute.

Serve the broccoli with sauce spooned over.

Note: Frozen broccoli may be used instead of fresh.

Above: Cabbage parcels; Broccoli with cheese sauce. Right: Stuffed onions; Stuffed jacket potatoes

STUFFED ONIONS

Serves 4 Cooking time: 10-12 minutes, plus standing
Microwave setting: Maximum (Full)

4 large onions, total weight 1 kg (2 lb), peeled
½ cup fresh white breadcrumbs
¼ teaspoon chopped sage
1 teaspoon chopped tarragon
1 teaspoon chopped parsley
1 teaspoon Worcestershire sauce
1 egg yolk, lightly beaten
salt
freshly ground black pepper
30 g (1 oz) butter

Remove the centres from the onions, using a grapefruit knife, leaving shells 2-3 layers deep. Chop the centres and mix with the remaining ingredients except butter.

Stuff each onion with the breadcrumb mixture and top with butter, reserving a little of it.

Arrange the onions in a circle on a plate and cook uncovered for 10-12 minutes, turning them round halfway through cooking. Leave to stand for 3 minutes. Melt remaining butter and use to brush onions before serving.

STUFFED JACKET POTATOES

Serves 4 Cooking time: 13-16 minutes, plus standing
Microwave setting: Maximum (Full)

4 medium potatoes, washed and dried
¾ cup grated Cheddar cheese
1 tablespoon tomato paste
1 tablespoon Worcestershire sauce
15 g (½ oz) butter
salt
freshly ground black pepper
chopped parsley, to garnish

Place the potatoes on a paper towel, prick them and cook for 6 minutes.

Turn the potatoes over and turn the paper towel round. Cook for a further 4-7 minutes.

Wrap each potato tightly in foil and leave to stand for 5 minutes.

Cut a slice off a long side of each potato. Scoop out the flesh, leaving the potato shell intact.

Mix the potato flesh with the cheese, tomato paste, Worcestershire sauce, butter, salt and pepper.

Pile the mixture back into the potato jackets and reheat for 3 minutes. Serve sprinkled with parsley.

ZUCCHINI SHELLS WITH BACON

Serves 4 Cooking time: 12 minutes, plus standing
Microwave setting: Maximum (Full)

- 4 zucchini, halved lengthwise
- 1 bacon rasher, rind removed and chopped
- 1 small onion, peeled and finely chopped
- 1 teaspoon chopped oregano
- ½-1 cup fresh white breadcrumbs
- 1 egg yolk
- 4 tablespoons stock
- salt
- freshly ground black pepper

Using a teaspoon, scoop the centres from the zucchini halves. Set the shells aside, chop the flesh and place it with the bacon, onion and oregano in a small bowl. Cover and cook for 3 minutes. Stir in the breadcrumbs, egg yolk, stock, salt and pepper.

Fill 4 of the shells with stuffing, mounding it. Top with remaining shells, pressing on lightly.

Place in a shallow dish, cover and cook for 9 minutes, rearranging halfway through cooking. Leave to stand for 3-4 minutes.

STUFFED MARROW

Serves 4 Cooking time: 26½-29½ minutes
Microwave setting: Maximum (Full)

- 1 small marrow, about 750 g (1½ lb), halved and seeds removed
- 1 medium onion, peeled and finely chopped
- 1 small carrot, peeled and grated
- 2 tomatoes, skinned and chopped
- 1 teaspoon chopped basil or oregano
- 1½ cups fresh brown breadcrumbs
- 375 g (12 oz) minced beef
- 1 teaspoon Worcestershire sauce
- 2 teaspoons tomato paste
- salt
- freshly ground black pepper
- paprika (optional)

Sauce:

- 30 g (1 oz) butter
- 2 tablespoons plain flour
- 1¼ cups milk
- salt
- freshly ground black pepper

Place the marrow in a shallow dish. Cover and cook for 8-10 minutes. Drain, cover and set aside.

Place the vegetables and basil or oregano in a large bowl. Cover and cook for 5 minutes. Stir in the breadcrumbs, meat, Worcestershire sauce, tomato paste, salt and pepper. Cover and cook 4 minutes.

To make the sauce, place the butter in a bowl. Cook for 1 minute or until melted. Blend in the flour, cook 1 minute then stir in the milk. Cook for 4-5 minutes, stirring every minute. Season with salt and pepper.

Fill the marrow halves with the stuffing. Spoon over the sauce and cook for 3½ minutes. Sprinkle with paprika or **brown under a preheated conventional grill** before serving if preferred.

Clockwise: Peppers with savoury rice; Stuffed eggplant; Stuffed marrow; Zucchini shells with bacon

PEPPERS WITH SAVOURY RICE

Serves 4 Cooking time: 23 minutes, plus standing
Microwave setting: Maximum (Full)

1 onion, peeled and finely chopped
30 g (1 oz) butter
60 g (2 oz) ham, finely chopped
1 garlic clove, peeled and crushed
2 teaspoons tomato paste
1 tablespoon chopped parsley
salt
freshly ground black pepper
¾ cup long-grain rice
1¼ cups hot beef stock
4 green peppers, tops cut off, cored, seeded and blanched for 2 minutes in boiling water

Place the onion, butter, ham, garlic, tomato paste, parsley, salt and pepper in a large bowl. Cover and cook for 4 minutes.

Stir in the rice and stock, cover and cook for 9 minutes. Leave to stand, covered, for about 10 minutes.

Stand the peppers in a casserole. Stuff them with the rice, cover and cook for 5 minutes.

Turn each pepper round and cook for 5 minutes. Stand, covered, for 5 minutes before serving.

STUFFED EGGPLANT

Serves 4 Cooking time: 15¾ minutes
Microwave setting: Maximum (Full)

2 medium eggplant, about 275 g (9 oz) each
salt
oil, for brushing
1 medium onion, peeled and finely chopped
4 streaky bacon rashers, rinds removed, diced
60 g (2 oz) mushrooms, chopped
125 g (4 oz) butter
2 tablespoons tomato paste
1 tablespoon chopped parsley
2 teaspoons Worcestershire sauce
dash of Angostura bitters (optional)
1 garlic clove, peeled and crushed
freshly ground black pepper
1½ cups brown breadcrumbs
½ cup finely grated Cheddar cheese

Cut the eggplant in half lengthwise. Sprinkle the cut sides with salt and set aside. After 30 minutes, rinse them with cold water and pat dry.

Scoop out flesh and dice it. Brush shells with oil.

Place the onion in a large bowl. Cover and cook for 2 minutes. Stir in the bacon and diced eggplant. Cover and cook for 4 minutes.

Stir in the mushrooms, butter, tomato paste, parsley, Worcestershire sauce, Angostura bitters (if using), garlic, salt and pepper. Cover and cook for 3 minutes. Leave to stand, covered.

Place the eggplant shells on a plate or shallow casserole dish, cover and cook for 2 minutes. Turn each shell round, cover and cook 2 minutes more.

Stir the breadcrumbs into the stuffing. Spoon the stuffing into the shells. Cook for 2 minutes.

Sprinkle the grated cheese on top and cook for 45 seconds or until the cheese has melted.

VEGETARIAN CURRY

Serves 4 Cooking time: 20 minutes
Microwave setting: Maximum (Full)

1 tablespoon vegetable oil
1 small green pepper, cored, seeded and finely chopped
2 carrots, peeled and finely sliced
1 celery stick, finely chopped
2 large onions, peeled and finely chopped
3 tomatoes, skinned and chopped
1 tablespoon lemon juice
1 large eating apple, peeled, cored and chopped
2 tablespoons brown sugar
2 tablespoons curry powder
2 teaspoons turmeric
2 tablespoons desiccated coconut
2 tablespoons plain flour
3 tablespoons water
1¼ cups hot vegetable stock
2 tablespoons sultanas
2 tablespoons peanuts
salt
freshly ground black pepper

Place the oil, green pepper, carrots and celery in a bowl. Cover and cook for 5 minutes.

Stir in the onions, tomatoes, lemon juice, apple, sugar, curry powder, turmeric and coconut. Cover and cook for 10 minutes, stirring halfway through.

Stir in the flour, blended with the water. Cook 1 minute, then stir in the hot stock, sultanas, peanuts, salt and pepper. Cover and cook for 4 minutes, stirring halfway through.

Serve with brown rice.

ONION & POTATO SCALLOP

Serves 4-6 Cooking time: 15-18 minutes
Microwave setting: Maximum (Full)

500 g (1 lb) onions, peeled and thinly sliced
600 g (1¼ lb) potatoes, peeled and thinly sliced
salt
freshly ground black pepper
nutmeg
scant ⅓ cup milk
parsley sprigs, to garnish

Place the onions in a medium bowl, cover and cook for 5 minutes, stirring halfway through cooking.

Layer the potatoes and onions in a shallow casserole dish. Sprinkle each layer with a little salt, black pepper and nutmeg. Finish off with a layer of potatoes. Pour in the milk.

Stand the dish on a plate. Cover and cook for 10-13 minutes, turning round halfway through cooking.

Garnish with parsley.

Clockwise: Salami and tomato pizza; Potato salad; Onion and potato scallop; Vegetarian curry

SALAMI & TOMATO PIZZA

Serves 4-6 Cooking time: about 11 minutes
Microwave setting: Maximum (Full)

2½ tablespoons milk
1 sachet (1½ teaspoons) dried yeast
pinch of caster sugar
30 g (1 oz) butter
1 egg, beaten
1½ cups plain flour, sifted with a pinch of salt

Topping:
1 garlic clove, peeled and crushed
1 medium onion, peeled and finely chopped
15 g (½ oz) butter
2 tablespoons tomato paste
375 g (12 oz) fresh tomatoes, skinned and chopped or drained, canned tomatoes
1 tablespoon chopped oregano
salt
freshly ground black pepper
90-125 g (3-4 oz) salami, thinly sliced
¾ cup grated Cheddar cheese
2 tablespoons grated Parmesan cheese
6 anchovies, drained
6 stuffed green olives, halved

Place the milk in a jug. Cook for 15 seconds. Sprinkle the yeast and sugar over the milk and leave to stand for 10 minutes or until frothy.

Place the butter in a small bowl. Cook for 45 seconds or until melted.

Pour the yeast mixture, melted butter and egg into the flour and salt. Knead for 10 minutes or until smooth. Shape into a ball and place in a bowl.

Cover and cook for 30 seconds. Leave covered for 10 minutes. Remove the cover and leave dough to rise for about 20 minutes or until it has doubled in size.

Place the garlic, onion and butter in a medium bowl. Cover and cook for 3 minutes. Stir in the tomato paste, tomatoes, oregano, salt and pepper. Cook for 2 minutes. Set aside.

Knead the dough and roll it out to make a 23 cm (9 inch) circle. Place on a plate or microwave pizza tray and cook for 2½ minutes. Spread the tomato mixture over the dough and cover with the salami and cheeses. Lattice the anchovies on top. Garnish with olives, cook for 2 minutes and serve immediately.

POTATO SALAD

Serves 4 Cooking time: 6-9 minutes
Microwave setting: Maximum (Full)

750 g (1½ lb) potatoes, peeled and cut into 1 cm (½ inch) cubes
salt
¾ cup mayonnaise
1 tablespoon snipped chives, to garnish

Place potatoes in a plastic bag, tie with string and prick the bag. Cook for 6-9 minutes until tender, turning bag once.

Leave to stand for 15 minutes. Remove potato and gently stir with a fork to separate the cubes. Season with salt if desired. Cool.

Fold in the mayonnaise and sprinkle with chives.

FLUFFY RICE

Serves 4 as an accompaniment Cooking time: 13 minutes, plus standing
Microwave setting: Maximum (Full)

1 cup long-grain rice
1¾ cups cold water or stock
¼ teaspoon oil
salt

Place rice in a lidded casserole and add liquid and oil. Cover with lid and cook 13 minutes. Stand, covered, 10 minutes. Add salt and fork up. For brown rice, follow directions but add 2½ cups liquid and cook 30 minutes.

From left to right: Fluffy rice; Spaghetti all'uova; Buttered spaghetti; Cooked lentils

BUTTERED SPAGHETTI

Serves 3-4 Cooking time: 9 minutes
Microwave setting: Maximum (Full)

salt
1 tablespoon oil
7 cups boiling water
250 g (8 oz) spaghetti
125 g (4 oz) butter, cut into pieces

Place the salt, oil and water in a large bowl. Stand the spaghetti in the water and cook uncovered for 1 minute.

Gently push the remaining spaghetti under the water. Cover and cook for 8 minutes. Check during cooking that all the spaghetti is completely submerged.

Leave to stand, covered, for 10 minutes. Drain and toss in the butter.

RICE, PASTA & PULSES

SPAGHETTI ALL'UOVA

Serves 3-4 Cooking time: 9 minutes, plus standing
Microwave setting: Maximum (Full)

250 g (8 oz) spaghetti
salt
1 tablespoon oil
7 cups boiling water
3 eggs, lightly beaten
125 g (4 oz) butter, cut into pieces
½ cup grated pecorino cheese

Cook the spaghetti in the salt, oil and water as in Buttered Spaghetti (see left).

Leave to stand, covered, for 10 minutes. Drain and toss in the beaten eggs until set.

Place half the butter in a serving bowl. Pile in the spaghetti and dot with the remaining butter.

Serve sprinkled with the grated cheese.

COOKED LENTILS

Serves 6 as an accompaniment
Cooking time: about 21 minutes, plus standing
Microwave setting: Maximum (Full) and Defrost

1¼ cups red lentils
60 g (2 oz) butter, cut into pieces

Place the lentils in a medium bowl with cold water to cover. Cover and cook at Maximum for 6 minutes or until boiling.

Turn to Defrost and cook for 15 minutes. Stand, covered, for 10 minutes before serving.

Drain and toss in butter.

KEDGEREE

Serves 6 Cooking time: 23½ minutes, plus standing
Microwave setting: Maximum (Full)

750 g (1½ lb) smoked cod or haddock fillets
2 cups long-grain rice
3½ cups hot chicken stock
salt
1 teaspoon oil
60 g (2 oz) butter, cut into cubes
1 egg, beaten
2 hard-boiled eggs, chopped
freshly ground black pepper
1 tablespoon cream

To garnish:
chopped parsley
1 hard-boiled egg white, chopped
1 hard-boiled egg yolk, sieved

Place the fish in a freezer bag, tie with string and prick the bag. Cook for 7½ minutes. Stand for 2-3 minutes. Flake the fish, discarding skin and bones. Set aside.

Place the rice, hot stock, salt and oil in a large bowl. Cover and cook for 12 minutes. Leave to stand, covered, for 7 minutes.

Stir the flaked fish into the rice with the butter, beaten egg, chopped hard-boiled egg, pepper and cream. Cover and cook for 4 minutes, stirring halfway through cooking.

Garnish with the chopped parsley, chopped egg white and sieved egg yolk, arranged decoratively over the kedgeree.

CURRIED RICE

Serves 6 Cooking time: 17 minutes, plus standing
Microwave setting: Maximum (Full)

30 g (1 oz) ghee
1 large onion, peeled and finely chopped
1 garlic clove, peeled and crushed
2 cups long-grain rice
1 tablespoon mild curry powder
1 teaspoon Mexican-style chilli powder
½ cup sultanas
1 tablespoon tomato paste
5 cm (2 inch) piece cinnamon stick
small piece bay leaf
salt
¼ teaspoon oil
2½ cups boiling beef stock
bay leaves, to garnish

Place the ghee, onion, garlic, rice, curry powder and chilli powder in a large bowl, cover and cook for 5 minutes, stirring halfway through cooking.

Stir in the remaining ingredients except bay leaves for garnish. Cover and cook for 12 minutes. Stand, covered, for 8 minutes.

Fluff the rice with a fork, remove cinnamon and bay leaf. Serve garnished with bay leaves.

Clockwise: Risotto; Paella; Curried rice; Kedgeree

RISOTTO

Serves 6 Cooking time: 21-22 minutes, plus standing
Microwave setting: Maximum (Full)

60 g (2 oz) butter
1 large onion, peeled and finely chopped
1 garlic clove, peeled and crushed
2 cups long-grain rice
¼ green pepper, cored, seeded and finely diced
¼ red pepper, cored, seeded and finely diced
2 teaspoons tomato paste
4½ cups hot chicken stock
125 g (4 oz) ham, finely chopped
¼ teaspoon oil
salt
freshly ground black pepper
60 g (2 oz) mushrooms, sliced
1 tablespoon lemon juice
1 tablespoon chopped parsley, to garnish
grated Parmesan cheese, to serve

Place the butter, onion, garlic and rice in a large bowl. Cover and cook for 5-6 minutes, stirring halfway through cooking.

Stir in the peppers, tomato paste, stock, ham, oil, salt and pepper, then cover and cook for 14 minutes, stirring halfway through. Stand, covered, for 8 minutes.

Sprinkle the mushrooms with lemon juice and cook in a covered bowl for 2 minutes. Add to the risotto and fold through with a fork. Sprinkle with chopped parsley. Hand grated Parmesan cheese separately.

PAELLA

Serves 6 Cooking time: 23½ minutes, plus standing
Microwave setting: Maximum (Full)

1 tablespoon oil
1 large onion, peeled and chopped
2 garlic cloves, peeled and crushed
2 cups long-grain rice
3½ cups boiling chicken stock
pinch of saffron
salt
125 g (4 oz) frozen peas
185 g (6 oz) cooked peeled prawns
185 g (6 oz) cooked mussels
250 g (8 oz) cooked chicken meat, diced
2 tomatoes, peeled and chopped
cooked prawns in shells, to garnish

Place the oil, onion and garlic in a large shallow bowl, cover and cook for 2 minutes, stirring halfway through.

Stir in the rice, stock and saffron. Cover and cook for 12 minutes, stirring halfway through. Set aside, covered, for 8 minutes, then add salt if necessary and fluff up with a fork.

Meanwhile place the peas in a medium bowl, cover and cook for 2 minutes. Stir in the prawns, mussels, chicken and tomatoes. Cover and cook for 7½ minutes, stirring halfway through. Drain and arrange over the rice. Serve hot, garnished with prawns.

SPAGHETTI BOLOGNESE

Serves 3-4 Cooking time: 20½ minutes
Microwave setting: Maximum (Full)

1 quantity cooked spaghetti (see page 112)
4 streaky bacon rashers, rinds removed, chopped
1 medium onion, peeled and finely chopped
2 garlic cloves, peeled and crushed
1 celery stick, finely chopped
1 small carrot, peeled and grated
2 tablespoons plain flour
250 g (8 oz) minced steak
500 g (1 lb) tomatoes, skinned and chopped, or 1×410 g can tomatoes, undrained
3 tablespoons tomato paste
1¼ cups hot beef stock
125 g (4 oz) mushrooms, chopped
salt
freshly ground black pepper
2 tablespoons chopped mixed parsley and basil

Cook the spaghetti in the salt, oil and water as in Buttered Spaghetti (see page 112).

Place the bacon, onion, garlic, celery and carrot in a bowl. Cover and cook for 7½ minutes, stirring halfway through.

Stir in the flour, minced steak, tomatoes and tomato paste. Cover and cook for 3 minutes.

Stir in the stock, mushrooms, salt, pepper and herbs. Cover. Cook for 10 minutes, stirring after 5.

STUFFED CANNELLONI

Serves 4 Cooking time: about 28 minutes, plus standing
Microwave setting: Maximum (Full)

8 instant cannelloni tubes

Stuffing:
1 small onion, peeled and finely chopped
1 garlic clove, peeled and crushed
1 teaspoon chopped basil
1 teaspoon chopped oregano
250 g (8 oz) minced beef or pork
1 tablespoon tomato paste
salt
freshly ground black pepper

Sauce:
1 small onion, peeled and finely chopped
1 garlic clove, peeled and crushed
2 tablespoons chopped parsley
30 g (1 oz) butter, cut into pieces
1½ tablespoons plain flour
1×410 g can tomatoes
2 tablespoons tomato paste
salt
freshly ground black pepper

Make the stuffing first. Place the onion, garlic and herbs in a bowl. Cover and cook for 4 minutes. Stir in the meat, tomato paste, salt and pepper. Cover and cook 4 minutes, stirring once. Set aside.

To make the sauce, place the onion, garlic and parsley in a medium bowl. Cover and cook for 4 minutes. Stir in the butter until melted. Stir in the flour and cook 1 minute. Blend in the remaining ingredients. Cook uncovered for 4 minutes, stirring once. Puree in a blender.

Stuff the cannelloni with the meat stuffing. Place in a shallow casserole and pour sauce over. Cook, covered with plastic film left open at one side, for 10 minutes. Stand 3-4 minutes before serving.

HAM & CHICKEN LASAGNE

Serves 4 Cooking time: 26 minutes
Microwave setting: Maximum (Full)

375 g (12 oz) chicken pieces
1 medium onion, peeled and finely chopped
1 small green pepper, cored, seeded and finely chopped
45 g (1½ oz) butter
3 tablespoons plain flour
1¼ cups milk
½ cup hot chicken stock
60 g (2 oz) cooked ham, finely chopped
salt
freshly ground black pepper
185 g (6 oz) green instant lasagne
3 tablespoons grated Pecorino cheese
1 tablespoon grated Parmesan cheese
paprika (optional)

Place the chicken in a shallow dish. Cover and cook for 6 minutes. Set aside, covered, for 5 minutes. Discard skin and bones, chop flesh. Set aside.

Place the onion, green pepper and butter in a medium bowl. Cover and cook for 3 minutes, stir in the flour and cook 1 minute.

Stir in the milk and cook for 4 minutes. Stir in the stock, chicken, ham, salt and pepper. Cook for 2 minutes.

Layer the sauce and lasagne in a 5 cm (2 inch) deep oblong dish, beginning and ending with sauce. Cover the dish with plastic film left open at one side and cook for 8 minutes. Remove plastic, sprinkle cheese and paprika over and cook for 2 minutes or until the cheese has melted. **If preferred, omit paprika and brown under a preheated conventional grill.**

MACARONI CHEESE

Serves 3-4 Cooking time: 19-21 minutes
Microwave setting: Maximum (Full)

5 cups boiling water
¼ teaspoon oil
250 g (8 oz) macaroni

Sauce:
60 g (2 oz) butter
4 tablespoons plain flour
2½ cups milk
½ teaspoon prepared English mustard
salt
freshly ground black pepper
1¼ cups finely grated Cheddar cheese
paprika (optional)

Place the water, oil and macaroni in a large bowl. Cover and cook for 10 minutes. Set aside, covered.

Place the butter in a bowl. Cook uncovered for 1 minute or until melted. Stir in the flour and cook 1 minute, then blend in the milk, mustard, salt and pepper. Cook uncovered for 5-7 minutes, stirring every minute. Stir in ¾ cup of cheese. Drain macaroni and fold in. Pour into a casserole.

Sprinkle over the remaining cheese and paprika, if using. Cook uncovered for 2 minutes, or until cheese has melted. If preferred, omit paprika and **brown under a preheated conventional grill.**

Clockwise: Spaghetti Bolognese; Macaroni cheese; Stuffed cannelloni; Ham and chicken lasagne

Apple and sultana suet pudding;
Apple and berry crumble

APPLE & SULTANA SUET PUDDING

Serves 4-6 Cooking time: 11 minutes, plus standing
Microwave setting: Maximum (Full)

155 g (5 oz) shredded suet
½ teaspoon baking powder
1¼ cups self-raising flour
½ cup water
½ cup fresh brown breadcrumbs
½ cup brown sugar
2 teaspoons ground cinnamon
¾ cup sultanas
600 g (1¼ lb) cooking apples, peeled, cored and thinly sliced

Place the suet, baking powder and flour in a bowl. Mix together. Gradually stir in water to make pastry. Roll out ⅔ of the pastry to 3 mm (⅛ inch) thick and line a greased 5-cup basin.

Mix together the breadcrumbs, sugar, cinnamon and sultanas.

Starting and ending with the apples, make alternate layers with the breadcrumb mixture.

Roll out the remaining pastry and cover the filling, pressing edges of the lid and sides together to seal well. Make 2 cuts in the lid.

Cook for 5 minutes. Turn the basin round and cook for a further 6 minutes.

Leave to stand, covered with a teatowel, for 5 minutes before turning out and serving.

PUDDINGS & CAKES

APPLE & BERRY CRUMBLE

Serves 4-6 Cooking time: 12 minutes, plus standing
Microwave setting: Maximum (Full)

600 g (1¼ lb) cooking apples, peeled, cored and thinly sliced
375 g (12 oz) fresh or frozen thawed blackberries or boysenberries
⅓ cup white sugar
¾ cup plain flour
¾ cup desiccated coconut
½ cup brown sugar
90 g (3 oz) butter, melted

Layer the apples, blackberries and white sugar in a shallow dish. Mix the remaining ingredients together and sprinkle the mixture over the fruit.

Cook uncovered for 12 minutes. Leave to stand for 3 minutes before serving.

TREACLE PUDDING

Serves 4 Cooking time: 4 minutes, plus standing
Microwave setting: Maximum (Full)

3 tablespoons golden syrup
1 cup self-raising flour
60 g (2 oz) shredded suet
¼ cup caster sugar
1 egg
2 tablespoons water
4 tablespoons milk
2 drops vanilla essence

Place the golden syrup in the bottom of a lightly greased 4-cup basin.

Mix the flour, suet and sugar together. Mix the egg, water, milk and vanilla essence and beat in. Turn the mixture on to the syrup in the basin.

Cover the basin with plastic film and cook for 2 minutes. Remove the plastic film and turn the basin round. Cook for a further 2 minutes.

Leave the pudding to stand, covered, for 2 minutes before turning out and serving.

COLD STRAWBERRY SOUFFLE

Serves 6 Cooking time: 30 seconds
Microwave setting: Maximum (Full)

2 tablespoons white wine
4 tablespoons water
1½ tablespoons gelatine
1¼ cups pureed strawberries
1½ tablespoons lemon juice
½ cup caster sugar
1¼ cups cream, stiffly whipped
6 egg whites, stiffly whisked

To decorate:
1¼ cup cream, stiffly whipped
6 strawberries

Tie doubled greaseproof paper around the outside of 6 individual souffle dishes so that it extends 2.5 cm (1 inch) above the rim.

Place the wine, water, and gelatine in a small bowl. Stir together well and cook for 30 seconds. Stir to ensure the gelatine has dissolved.

Add the strawberry puree, lemon juice and sugar to the gelatine mixture and stir well. Allow to cool, stirring once or twice.

Carefully fold the cream into the strawberry mixture, then gently fold in the egg whites. Spoon mixture into the prepared dishes.

Chill until set, then remove the paper and decorate each souffle with piped whipped cream and a strawberry.

Treacle pudding; Cold strawberry souffle

CHRISTMAS PUDDING

Serves 6-8 Cooking time: 10 minutes, plus standing
Microwave setting: Maximum (Full)

¾ cup plain flour
¼ teaspoon salt
90 g (3 oz) shredded suet
½ teaspoon mixed spice
¼ teaspoon ground cinnamon
¾ cup fresh wholemeal breadcrumbs
¼ cup caster sugar
60 g (2 oz) mixed peel
⅓ cup brown sugar
60 g (2 oz) glace cherries, chopped
90 g (3 oz) currants
90 g (3 oz) sultanas
125 g (4 oz) raisins
45 g (1½ oz) blanched almonds, chopped
60 g (2 oz) chopped apple
juice of ½ lemon
grated rind of ½ lemon
4 tablespoons brandy
2 eggs
¼ cup medium sherry
2 teaspoons golden syrup
1 teaspoon Parisian essence

This pudding tastes best when freshly made. As it only takes 10 minutes to cook, it is easily fitted into the Christmas lunch schedule. See page 89. Do not put any silver pieces or coins into the mixture.

Mix all the dry ingredients together, then stir in the liquids.

Place the mixture in a 7-cup greased pudding basin. Cover the basin and cook for 5 minutes.

Leave to stand for 5 minutes, then cook for a further 5 minutes.

Allow the pudding to stand for 5 minutes.

QUEEN OF PUDDINGS

Serves 4-6 Cooking time: 13½ minutes, plus grilling
Microwave setting: Maximum (Full)

3 egg yolks
¼ cup caster sugar
2½ cups milk
2 drops vanilla essence
3 cups fresh white breadcrumbs
grated rind of ½ lemon
2 tablespoons jam

Topping:
¾ cup caster sugar
3 egg whites, stiffly whisked

Place the egg yolks, caster sugar, milk and vanilla essence in a bowl and whisk together. Cook for 4 minutes.

Place the breadcrumbs and grated lemon rind in a greased, shallow 5-cup heatproof dish and stir in the milk mixture. Cook for 5½ minutes, stirring every minute. Set aside.

Place the jam in a small dish. Cook for 1 minute.

Gently spread the jam over the cooked breadcrumb and milk mixture.

For the topping, fold the sugar into the whisked egg whites. Spread the meringue over the jam and swirl into decorative peaks. Cook 3 minutes.

Brown the pudding for a few moments under a preheated conventional grill.

Christmas pudding; Queen of puddings

FRUIT-STUFFED PANCAKES

Serves 4 Cooking time: 7½-10½ minutes, plus standing and pancakes
Microwave setting: Maximum (Full)

1 egg
1 egg yolk
1¼ cups milk
1 cup plain flour
pinch of salt
oil, for frying pancakes

Filling:
185 g (6 oz) dried apricots
2 cups cold water
2 drops almond essence
juice of 1 lemon
½ cup ground almonds
2 tablespoons caster sugar
2 tablespoons icing sugar

Beat together the egg, egg yolk and milk.

Sift the flour and salt into a large bowl. Make a well in the centre, add egg mixture and stir, gradually incorporating flour into liquid to make a batter. **Using a conventional stove-top,** heat a little oil in a 15 cm (6 inch) frying pan. Pour a little batter into the pan, swirling it to cover base. Cook until golden, turn and cook the other side. Make 8 pancakes in this way and set aside.

Place the apricots in a bowl and cover with cold water. Cover and cook for 5-10 minutes. Leave to stand, covered, for 20 minutes.

Drain the apricots and sieve or puree in a food processor.

Mix together the apricot puree, almond essence, lemon juice, ground almonds and caster sugar. Spread a little of the mixture in the centre of each pancake and roll up.

Arrange 4 pancakes on a plate and cook for 2½ minutes. Repeat with the remaining pancakes. Sift icing sugar over before serving.

BAKED STUFFED APPLES

Serves 4 Cooking time: 7-12 minutes, plus standing
Microwave setting: Maximum (Full)

3 tablespoons fruit mincemeat
3 tablespoons strawberry jam
1 teaspoon ground cinnamon
4 large cooking apples, total weight 1.25 kg (2½ lb), cored, skin scored around middle

Mix the mincemeat, jam and cinnamon together.

Stand the apples in a shallow dish. Spoon the filling into the cavities in the apples.

Cook, turning each apple round several times, for 7-12 minutes, until tender when tested with a fine skewer. Stand for 4 minutes before serving.

Fruit-stuffed pancakes; Baked stuffed apples

MIXED FRUIT SPONGE PUDDING

Serves 4 Cooking time: 6 minutes, plus standing
Microwave setting: Maximum (Full)

125 g (4 oz) butter
¾ cup caster sugar
2 eggs
1½ cups self-raising flour
2 tablespoons water
60 g (2 oz) mixed, dried fruit

Cream the butter and sugar together until light and fluffy. Beat in the eggs one at a time, then fold in the flour. Stir in the water and dried fruit.

Place the mixture in a greased 5-cup bowl. Cover and cook for 3 minutes. Turn the bowl and cook for a further 3 minutes.

Remove the cover and leave the pudding to stand for 2 minutes before turning it out. Serve hot.

HONEY CHEESECAKE

Serves 6 Cooking time: 5 minutes
Microwave setting: Maximum (Full)

1 tablespoon golden syrup
125 g (4 oz) butter
250 g (8 oz) Granita biscuits, crushed
375 g (12 oz) cream cheese, softened (page 14)
½ teaspoon ground cinnamon
1 tablespoon lemon juice
2 tablespoons water
1 tablespoon gelatine
4 tablespoons honey
½ cup cream, whipped

To decorate:
½ cup cream, whipped
walnut halves

Place the syrup and butter in a medium bowl. Cook for 1¼ minutes. Stir in the crushed biscuits and mix well. Use this mixture to line a 20 cm (8 inch) non-metal flan case. Cook 3 minutes. Cool.

Beat the cream cheese and cinnamon together until smooth.

Place lemon juice and water in a jug and stir in the gelatine. Cook for 15 seconds. Stir well to make sure the gelatine has dissolved.

Place the honey in another jug. Cook for 30 seconds and pour into the gelatine mixture. Mix well together. Cool slightly.

Beat the honey mixture into the cheese mixture and fold in the whipped cream. Spoon into the flan case and chill until set.

Decorate the cheesecake with the whipped cream and walnut halves.

Mixed fruit sponge pudding; Honey cheesecake

CHOCOLATE MOUSSE

Serves 6 Cooking time: about 2 minutes
Microwave setting: Maximum (Full)

6 slices jam Swiss roll
4 tablespoons Grand Marnier
250 g (8 oz) milk chocolate, broken into pieces
30 g (1 oz) butter
1 tablespoon cold strong black coffee
1 tablespoon brandy
4 egg yolks
4 egg whites, stiffly whisked

To decorate:
½ cup cream, stiffly whipped
1 tablespoon grated chocolate

Place Swiss roll slices into the bases of 6 small dishes. Sprinkle with the Grand Marnier.

Place the chocolate in a medium bowl. Cook for 2 minutes or until it has melted.

Beat in the butter, coffee, brandy and egg yolks. Gently fold in the egg whites.

Spoon the mousse over the Swiss roll and smooth over the top. Chill until set.

Decorate each dish with swirls of cream and grated chocolate.

PINEAPPLE FLAN

Serves 4-6 Cooking time: about 5½ minutes
Microwave setting: Maximum (Full)

125 g (4 oz) butter, cut into pieces
1 tablespoon golden syrup
250 g (8 oz) gingernut biscuits, crushed
4 tablespoons pineapple juice
4½ teaspoons gelatine
1×450 g can crushed pineapple, drained
60 g (2 oz) white marshmallows
1¼ cups cream, whipped

To decorate:
glace cherries
crystallized angelica, cut into leaf shapes

Place the butter and syrup in a medium bowl. Cook for 1¼ minutes. Stir in the crushed biscuits and mix well. Use this mixture to line a 20 cm (8 inch) non-metal flan case. Cook for 3 minutes.

Mix the pineapple juice and gelatine in a jug. Cook for 10 seconds, then stir until dissolved.

Place the crushed pineapple and marshmallows in a medium bowl. Cook for 1 minute or until the marshmallows have melted.

Whisk the pineapple juice and gelatine mixture into the pineapple and marshmallow mixture. Leave until almost set.

Fold the cream into the pineapple mixture and then spoon into the flan case, smoothing the top.

Decorate the flan with the cherries and angelica. Chill until set. Serve chilled.

TRIFLE

Serves 6 Cooking time: 5½ minutes
Microwave setting: Maximum (Full)

1×18 cm (7 inch) sponge, cut into pieces
12 sponge fingers, crumbled
½ cup sweet sherry
¼ cup orange juice
4 tablespoons strawberry jam
5 teaspoons caster sugar
1½ cups milk
3 eggs
1 egg yolk
½ cup cream, whipped
1 egg white, stiffly whisked

To decorate:
chopped nuts
angelica

Divide the sponge among 6 small glass dishes or place in 1 large dish. Sprinkle the sponge finger crumbs over the sponge.

Mix the sherry and orange juice together and pour over the sponge base. Spread a little strawberry jam over the soaked base.

Place the caster sugar and milk in a small bowl. Cook for 2 minutes.

Whisk the eggs and egg yolk together, then pour the heated milk on to the eggs, whisking all the time. Cook uncovered for 3½ minutes, checking and whisking the custard every 30 seconds.

Whisk and strain the custard before spooning it over the soaked sponge bases. Leave to cool.

Fold the cream and egg white together. Gently spread over the custard and decorate the trifle with chopped nuts and angelica.

PINEAPPLE UPSIDE DOWN PUDDING

Serves 4-6 Cooking time: 7-8 minutes, plus standing
Microwave setting: Maximum (Full)

170 g (5½ oz) butter
2 tablespoons brown sugar
3 slices canned pineapple
4 glace cherries
½ cup caster sugar
2 eggs
1 cup self-raising flour, sifted

Use 15 g (½ oz) of the butter to grease a 5-cup souffle dish. Place 30 g (1 oz) of butter and the brown sugar in the dish and cook for 1 minute. Spread over the base of the dish.

Arrange the pineapple slices and cherries over the butter and sugar in a decorative pattern.

Beat the remaining butter and caster sugar together until light and fluffy.

Beat in the eggs and fold in the flour. Gently spread this over the pineapple and cherries.

Cook for 3 minutes, turn the dish round and cook for further 3-4 minutes.

Leave the pudding to stand, loosely covered, for 3 minutes before turning out.

Clockwise: Trifle; Chocolate mousse; Pineapple upside down pudding; Pineapple flan

FRESH FRUIT SALAD

Serves 6 Cooking time: 5 minutes
Microwave setting: Maximum (Full)

½ cup sugar
½ cup water
1 tablespoon lemon juice
1 tablespoon Grand Marnier
60 g (2 oz) white grapes, peeled, halved and seeded
60 g (2 oz) black grapes, peeled, halved and seeded
1 apple, peeled, cored, quartered and thinly sliced
1 pear, peeled, cored and sliced
1 large orange, cut into skinless segments
1 paw paw, peeled, seeded and diced
¼ honeydew melon, skin removed, seeded and diced
1 kiwi fruit, peeled and sliced
1 banana, peeled and sliced

Place the sugar and water in a bowl and cover. Heat for 5 minutes, then stir. Cool syrup, then stir in the lemon juice and Grand Marnier.

Place the fruit in a glass bowl. Pour the syrup over and chill, covered, for 1 hour to let the flavours mingle.

BAKED BANANAS

Serves 4 Cooking time: 4 minutes
Microwave setting: Maximum (Full)

4 bananas, peeled and sliced
4 tablespoons rum
4 tablespoons orange juice
60 g (2 oz) gingernut biscuits, crushed
3 tablespoons brown sugar
½ cup cream

Place the sliced bananas in a glass dish, mix the rum and orange juice together and pour over.

Mix the biscuits and sugar together and sprinkle over the bananas.

Cook uncovered for 2 minutes. Turn the dish round and cook for a further 2 minutes.

Pour the cream over the baked bananas. Serve immediately.

From left to right: Fresh fruit salad; Baked bananas; Lemon meringue pie; Ginger sponge pudding

LEMON MERINGUE PIE

Serves 4 Cooking time: 9-10½ minutes, plus browning
Microwave setting: Maximum (Full)

185 g (6 oz) prepared shortcrust pastry
finely grated rind of 2 lemons
½ cup lemon juice
2 tablespoons cornflour
1 cup caster sugar
2 egg yolks, beaten
2 egg whites, stiffly whisked

Roll out the pastry and use it to line a 15 cm (6 inch) tart plate. Prick the pastry all over with a fork and cook for 4-5 minutes, or until crisp.

Make up the lemon rind and juice with cold water to 1¼ cups.

Mix the cornflour in a bowl with a little of the lemon water, then gradually stir in the remaining liquid. Cook for 3½ minutes or until the mixture thickens, stirring every minute.

Whisk ⅓ cup of the sugar with the egg yolks. Beat into the lemon mixture. Pour into the pastry case and leave to cool.

Place the whisked egg whites in a bowl and fold in the remaining sugar. Pile over the lemon filling. Cook for 1½-2 minutes.

Place under a preheated conventional grill for a few moments to brown the meringue.

GINGER SPONGE PUDDING

Serves 4 Cooking time: 6 minutes, plus standing
Microwave setting: Maximum (Full)

125 g (4 oz) butter
½ cup caster sugar
2 eggs
1 cup self-raising flour, sifted
2 teaspoons ground ginger
5 pieces preserved ginger, drained and sliced

Cream the butter and sugar together until light and fluffy.

Beat in the eggs, one at a time, then fold in the sifted flour and ground ginger.

Arrange the sliced ginger over the base of a greased 4-cup basin. Turn the pudding mixture into the basin over the ginger, smoothing the top.

Cook uncovered for 3 minutes. Turn the bowl round and cook for a further 3 minutes.

Leave the pudding to stand, covered, for 2 minutes before turning it out. Serve hot with Egg Custard (page 139) or Orange Sauce (page 139).

CHOCOLATE BANANA RING

Cooking time: 15 minutes, plus standing
Microwave setting: Maximum (Full)

2 eggs
4 tablespoons milk
1 cup brown sugar
125 g (4 oz) soft margarine
500 g (1 lb) bananas, peeled and chopped
2 cups self-raising flour
½ teaspoon baking powder
⅓ cup drinking chocolate powder

Icing:
⅓ cup icing sugar
⅓ cup drinking chocolate powder
1 tablespoon water

Put the eggs, milk, sugar, margarine and bananas into a food processor and process until smooth. Sift the dry ingredients into a large bowl. Stir in the banana mixture and mix thoroughly.

Spoon the mixture into a 9-cup ungreased, base-lined microwave baking ring. Cook for 5 minutes, turn the ring round and cook for a further 5 minutes.

Gently spread any uncooked cake mixture over the surface. Turn round and cook for 5 minutes.

Leave the ring to stand for 5 minutes before turning it out. Leave, covered, to cool completely.

Mix the sifted icing sugar and drinking chocolate. Quickly stir in the water. Spread icing over the top of the cake, drizzling some down the side.

ONE STAGE CHOCOLATE CAKE

Cooking time: 7-9 minutes, plus standing
Microwave setting: Maximum (Full)

185 g (6 oz) soft margarine
¾ cup caster sugar
⅓ cup cocoa powder
1¼ cups self-raising flour
1 teaspoon baking powder
2 drops vanilla essence
3 tablespoons milk
3 eggs
2 tablespoons icing sugar, to decorate

Place all the ingredients except the icing sugar in a large bowl. Beat well until the mixture is smooth, but be careful not to overbeat.

Spoon the mixture into an ungreased, base-lined 18 cm (7 inch) round, 9 cm (3½ inch) deep container. Stand on an upturned plate and cook for 3 minutes. Turn the container round and cook for a further 4-6 minutes.

Leave the cake to stand for 5 minutes before turning it out. Leave to cool completely.

Turn the cake out upside down on to a serving plate and sift icing sugar over the top to decorate.

LEMON SPONGE CAKE

Cooking time: 5-8 minutes, plus standing
Microwave setting: Maximum (Full)

2 cups self-raising flour
¼ teaspoon baking powder
125 g (4 oz) butter
¾ cup brown sugar
2 eggs
2 teaspoons grated lemon rind
1 tablespoon milk
2 teaspoons lemon juice
3 tablespoons Lemon Curd (page 132)
1½ cups icing sugar, sifted
2 tablespoons water
yellow food colouring
8 sugared lemon slices, to decorate

Sift the flour and baking powder into a large bowl. Rub in the butter until the mixture resembles breadcrumbs, then stir in the sugar.

Beat in the eggs, one at a time, then stir in the lemon rind, milk and lemon juice.

Spoon the mixture into an ungreased, base-lined 18 cm (7 inch) round, 9 cm (3½ inch) deep container. Stand on an upturned plate and cook for 2 minutes.

Turn the container round and cook for a further 2 minutes. Turn round again and cook for 1-3 minutes.

Leave the sponge to stand for 5 minutes before turning it out upside down on to a serving plate. Cover and leave to cool completely.

Split the cake into 2 layers. Spread one layer with the lemon butter and replace the other layer on top.

Mix the icing sugar with the water and yellow food colouring. Pour over the cake and decorate with lemon slices.

GINGERBREAD

Cooking time: 4½-5 minutes, plus standing
Microwave setting: Maximum (Full)

2 tablespoons treacle
3 teaspoons caster sugar
60 g (2 oz) butter
1 cup plain flour, sifted
½ teaspoon bicarbonate of soda
½ teaspoon ground mixed spice
½ teaspoon ground ginger
1 small egg

Place the treacle, sugar and butter in a medium bowl. Cook for 1½ minutes.

Allow the mixture to cool slightly, then stir in the dry ingredients. Beat in the egg.

Pour into an ungreased 6-cup deep oblong plastic container such as an icecream container. Stand on an upturned plate and cook for 3-3½ minutes, turning container round once.

Allow the gingerbread to stand, covered, for 5 minutes before turning out. Serve sliced and buttered.

Clockwise: Lemon sponge cake; Gingerbread; One stage chocolate cake; Chocolate banana ring

MULLED RED WINE

Serves 4 Cooking time: 4 minutes
Microwave setting: Maximum (Full)

2 cups red wine
½ cup water
½ cup orange juice
5 teaspoons caster sugar
4 tablespoons brandy
½ teaspoon ground cinnamon
8 orange slices, to decorate

Place all the ingredients except orange slices in a jug. Stir well and pour into 4 tumblers.

Heat for 4 minutes, stirring halfway through.

Decorate with the orange slices.

MULLED CIDER

Serves 4 Cooking time: 4 minutes
Microwave setting: Maximum (Full)

2 cups dry cider
½ cup apple juice
½ cup orange juice
5 teaspoons caster sugar
½ teaspoon ground mixed spice
8 apple slices

Place the cider, apple juice, orange juice, sugar and mixed spice into a large jug. Stir well and pour into 4 tumblers.

Place an apple slice in each tumbler. Heat for 4 minutes, stirring halfway through heating.

Decorate with the remaining apple slices.

From left to right: Mulled cider; Hot rum punch; Mulled red wine

DRINKS & PRESERVES

HOT RUM PUNCH

Serves 4 Cooking time: about 10 minutes
Microwave setting: Maximum (Full)

2 cups water
1 orange
6 cloves
2 tea bags
rind of ½ lemon
1 cinnamon stick
½ cup dark rum
½ cup white wine
½ cup orange juice
⅓ cup brown sugar

To decorate:
4 small slices orange
4 small slices lemon

Place the water in a large jug and cook for 5 minutes.

Stud the orange with the cloves and add to the water with the tea bags, lemon rind and cinnamon stick. Stir and cover, then set aside for 5 minutes, removing the tea bags after 3 minutes.

Place the rum, wine, orange juice and brown sugar in a jug. Cook for 5 minutes, stirring halfway through cooking.

Remove the orange and cloves, rind and cinnamon stick. Strain. Mix the tea and rum mixtures together, then pour into 4 heatproof or warmed glasses. Place a small slice of lemon and orange in each glass.

STRAWBERRY JAM

Makes about 500 g (1 lb) Cooking time: about 26 minutes
Microwave setting: Maximum (Full)

500 g (1 lb) small strawberries
2 tablespoons lemon juice
1½ cups sugar

Place the hulled strawberries and lemon juice in a large bowl. Cover and cook for 6 minutes.

Stir in the sugar and cook uncovered for 20 minutes or until setting point is reached, stirring halfway through. Allow the jam to cool then spoon into clean, dry jars. Seal and label.

LEMON CURD

Makes about 500 g (1 lb) Cooking time: about 8 minutes
Microwave setting: Maximum (Full)

125 g (4 oz) butter
1 cup sugar
6 tablespoons lemon juice
grated rind of 3 large lemons
3 eggs

Place the butter, sugar, lemon juice and rind in a large bowl. Cook uncovered for 3 minutes, stirring halfway through cooking.

Beat the eggs into the mixture. Cook for 5 minutes or until the lemon butter thickens, checking and stirring every 30 seconds.

Allow to cool before spooning into clean, dry jars. Seal and label.

From left to right: Strawberry jam; Lemon curd; Gooseberry jam; Tomato chutney

GOOSEBERRY JAM

Makes about 750 g (1 ½ lb) Cooking time: about 30 minutes
Microwave setting: Maximum (Full)

2 cups sugar
¾ cup water
500 g (1 lb) fresh or thawed, frozen gooseberries, topped and tailed

Place sugar in a bowl and heat for 30 seconds. Set aside. Place the water and gooseberries in a large bowl. Cover and cook for 5 minutes.

Stir the jam and cook uncovered 5 minutes or until gooseberries are soft. Stir in the sugar and cook uncovered 20 minutes or until setting point is reached, stirring halfway through cooking.

Allow the jam to cool before spooning into clean, dry jars. Seal and label.

TOMATO CHUTNEY

Makes about 1.5 kg (3 lb) Cooking time: about 34 minutes
Microwave setting: Maximum (Full)

375 g (12 oz) tomatoes, skinned and chopped
375 g (12 oz) cooking apples, peeled, cored and sliced
1 medium onion, peeled and finely chopped
375 g (12 oz) raisins
2 teaspoons salt
2 teaspoons mixed spice
1 garlic clove, peeled and crushed
1½ cups brown sugar
1¾ cups malt vinegar

Place the tomatoes, apples and onion in a large bowl. Cover and cook for 10 minutes, stirring halfway through cooking.

Stir in the raisins, salt, mixed spice, garlic, sugar and vinegar. Cook uncovered for 24 minutes, stirring the chutney several times during cooking.

Allow to cool before spooning into clean, dry jars. Seal and label.

HOT CHOCOLATE

Serves 4 Cooking time: about 8½ minutes
Microwave setting: Maximum (Full)

- 60 g (2 oz) dark chocolate, broken into pieces
- 2½ cups milk
- 5 marshmallows, chopped
- cinnamon or nutmeg (optional)

Place the chocolate in a large jug. Heat for 3½ minutes or until melted. Stir in the milk and heat for 4 minutes.

Whisk in the marshmallows until they have melted. Heat for 1 minute, then pour into 4 warmed mugs or glasses. If desired, dust with cinnamon or freshly grated nutmeg.

HOT WHISKY EGG NOG

Serves 4 Cooking time: 6 minutes
Microwave setting: Maximum (Full)

- 3 cups milk
- ¼ cup whisky
- ½ cup caster sugar
- 2 eggs, lightly beaten
- grated nutmeg, to decorate

Place the milk, whisky and sugar in a large jug. Cook for 6 minutes, stirring halfway through.

Beat a little of the hot milk mixture into the eggs, then beat this into the remaining mixture. Strain into 4 heatproof or warmed tumblers. Sprinkle grated nutmeg over each and serve immediately.

Hot chocolate; Hot whisky egg nog;
Calypso coffee; Orange tea

CALYPSO COFFEE

Serves 4 Cooking time: 4½ minutes
Microwave setting: Maximum (Full)

2½ cups cold, strong black coffee
5 teaspoons caster sugar
4 tablespoons rum
½ cup cream

Place the coffee, sugar and rum in a large jug. Heat for 4½ minutes, stirring halfway through.

Pour the coffee into 4 warmed glasses or cups.

Pour a little cream on the top of each coffee.

ORANGE TEA

Serves 4 Cooking time: 6 minutes
Microwave setting: Maximum (Full)

1 cup orange juice
2½ cups water
1 tablespoon caster sugar
2 tea bags

To decorate:
4 slices orange
4 mint sprigs

Place the orange juice, water and sugar in a large jug. Cook for 6 minutes, stirring halfway through cooking.

Stir in the tea bags, cover and leave to stand for 4 minutes.

Stir the orange tea, remove the tea bags, then pour into the 4 glasses and float a slice of orange on the top. Decorate each glass with a sprig of mint.

WHITE SAUCE

Makes 1½ cups Cooking time: 7½-9½ minutes
Microwave setting: Maximum (Full)

1 cup milk
1 slice onion
3-4 slices carrot
5 black peppercorns
1 small piece celery
30 g (1 oz) butter
1½ tablespoons plain flour
salt
freshly ground black pepper
pinch of nutmeg

Place the milk, onion, carrot, peppercorns and celery in a medium bowl and cook for 3 minutes. Leave to infuse 10 minutes then strain.

Place the butter in a bowl and cook for 30 seconds or until melted. Stir in the flour, cook 1-2 minutes, then gradually blend in the strained milk. Cook, stirring every minute, for 3-4 minutes or until thick and smooth. Stir in seasonings.

Variations:

Egg Sauce: Add 1 finely chopped hard-boiled egg. Serve with vegetables and fish.

Cheese Sauce: Stir ⅓ cup grated sharp Cheddar cheese into the sauce until it melts. Season with ½ teaspoon dry mustard and a pinch of cayenne. Serve with vegetables, pasta and fish.

Parsley Sauce: Add 2 tablespoons chopped fresh parsley. Serve with boiled bacon or fish.

Seafood Sauce: Add 2 tablespoons cooked peeled prawns, ½ teaspoon lemon juice or anchovy sauce and a pinch of paprika. Serve with vegetables or fish.

Caper Sauce: Add 1 tablespoon chopped capers and 1 tablespoon caper juice. Serve with chicken or fish.

From left to right: White sauce; Caper sauce; Egg sauce; Seafood sauce; Parsley sauce; Cheese sauce

SAUCES

JAM SAUCE

Makes ¾ cup Cooking time: 3 minutes
Microwave setting: Maximum (Full)

4 tablespoons jam
1 tablespoon lemon juice
4 tablespoons water

Place the jam, juice and water in a bowl. Cook for 3 minutes, stirring halfway through. Sieve the sauce if necessary.

Serve with rice pudding.

EGG CUSTARD

Makes about 1½ cups Cooking time: about 5 minutes
Microwave setting: Maximum (Full)

1¼ cups milk
2 drops vanilla essence
1 egg
1 egg yolk
¼ cup caster sugar
1½ teaspoons cornflour

Place the milk and vanilla essence in a jug and cook for 2 minutes.

Place the egg, egg yolk and sugar in a medium bowl and beat together. Add the cornflour to the mixture and beat until smooth.

Gradually stir the milk into the egg mixture.

Cook for 3 minutes, whisking every 30 seconds, until thick and smooth. Serve with steamed sponge pudding.

CHOCOLATE CUSTARD

Makes about 1½ cups Cooking time: about 3 minutes
Microwave setting: Maximum (Full)

1½ tablespoons cornflour
2 tablespoons cocoa powder
1½ tablespoons caster sugar
1¼ cups milk
15 g (½ oz) butter

Mix the cornflour, cocoa powder and sugar in a bowl. Gradually blend in the milk.

Cook for 3 minutes, stirring every minute, until thick and smooth. Beat in the butter and serve.

MELBA SAUCE

Makes 1 cup Cooking time: 2½ minutes
Microwave setting: Maximum (Full)

375 g (12 oz) fresh or thawed frozen raspberries, sieved
3 tablespoons caster sugar
2 teaspoons cornflour
1 tablespoon water
½ teaspoon lemon juice

Place the raspberries and sugar in a bowl. Blend the cornflour with the water and stir into the raspberries. Cook for 2½ minutes, stirring every minute.

Stir in the lemon juice, and allow to cool. Serve with ice cream.

ORANGE SAUCE

Makes about 1½ cups Cooking time: about 3½ minutes
Microwave setting: Maximum (Full)

90 g (3 oz) butter
1 cup icing sugar, sifted
¾ cup orange juice
1½ tablespoons cornflour
grated rind of 1 orange
1 egg, separated

Place the butter in a medium bowl, and cook for 1 minute or until melted. Beat the icing sugar into the melted butter.

Blend the orange juice and cornflour together and stir into the sugar mixture. Beat in the orange rind and egg yolk.

Cook for 2½ minutes or until thickened, stirring every 30 seconds. Cool.

Whisk the egg white into the orange sauce. Serve with marmalade pudding or Ginger Sponge Pudding (page 127).

GOOSEBERRY SAUCE

Makes about 2 cups Cooking time: 9 minutes
Microwave setting: Maximum (Full)

425 g (14 oz) fresh or thawed frozen gooseberries, topped and tailed
½ cup water
2 tablespoons cornflour
extra 1 tablespoon water
¼ cup caster sugar

Place the gooseberries and ½ cup water in a large bowl. Cover and cook for 6 minutes, stirring halfway through. Sieve or puree in a blender until smooth.

Beat together the cornflour and 1 tablespoon water. Stir in with the sugar and cook uncovered for 3 minutes, stirring halfway through.

This is the classic accompaniment to grilled mackerel and is also good with grilled mullet.

APPLE SAUCE

Makes about 1 cup Cooking time: about 8 minutes
Microwave setting: Maximum (Full)

2 tablespoons water
grated rind of ½ small lemon
1 tablespoon caster sugar
15 g (½ oz) butter
500 g (1 lb) cooking apples, peeled, cored and finely sliced

Place the water, lemon rind, sugar, butter and apples in a large bowl. Cover and cook for 5 minutes, stirring halfway through cooking. Cool the sauce slightly.

Pour into a blender and blend until smooth.

Return to the bowl and reheat for 3 minutes. Serve with roast pork.

Clockwise from top: Orange sauce; Gooseberry sauce; Apple sauce; Melba sauce; Chocolate custard; Jam sauce. Centre: Egg custard

SAUCE BEARNAISE

Makes about ½ cup Cooking time: about 1¾ minutes
Microwave setting: Maximum (Full)

90 g (3 oz) butter
2 tablespoons tarragon vinegar
1 tablespoon finely chopped onion
freshly ground black pepper
2 small egg yolks

To prevent curdling, check the sauce frequently during cooking. Serve with grilled steak.

Place the butter in a bowl and cook for 1 minute or until melted.

Whisk the tarragon vinegar, onion, pepper and egg yolks into the butter. Cook for 30-40 seconds, whisking the sauce every 10 seconds.

As soon as the sauce is ready, place the bowl in cold water to prevent further cooking.

CURRY SAUCE

Makes about 3 cups Cooking time: 12-14½ minutes
Microwave setting: Maximum (Full)

1 tablespoon ghee
1 medium onion, peeled and chopped
1 garlic clove, peeled and crushed
1 medium apple, peeled, cored and chopped
1 tablespoon ground coriander
1 teaspoon turmeric
½ teaspoon ground cumin
¼ teaspoon chilli powder
¼ teaspoon ground cinnamon
¼ teaspoon ground ginger
¼ teaspoon grated nutmeg
1½ tablespoons plain flour
1 tablespoon tomato paste
1 teaspoon lemon juice
2 teaspoons curry paste
2 cups hot stock
salt
freshly ground black pepper

Place the ghee, onion, garlic, apple, coriander, turmeric, cumin, chilli powder, cinnamon, ginger and nutmeg in a medium bowl. Cover and cook for 4½ minutes, stirring halfway through cooking.

Stir in the flour, tomato paste, lemon juice, curry paste, stock and salt and pepper to taste. Cover and cook for 8-10 minutes, stirring halfway through cooking.

ONION SAUCE

Makes about 1 cup Cooking time: 7 minutes
Microwave setting: Maximum (Full)

250 g (8 oz) onions, peeled and finely chopped
15 g (½ oz) butter
2 teaspoons cornflour
½ cup milk
salt
freshly ground black pepper

Place the onions and butter in a medium bowl, cover and cook for 5 minutes, stirring after 2.

Blend the cornflour with a little of the milk. Stir into the remaining milk, and add to the onions. Add the salt and pepper.

Cover and cook for 2 minutes, stirring once.

BREAD SAUCE

Makes about 1½ cups Cooking time: 7 minutes, plus standing
Microwave setting: Maximum (Full)

1 medium onion, peeled and stuck with 8 cloves
about 1¼ cups milk
1½ cups fresh white breadcrumbs
½ teaspoon nutmeg
60 g (2 oz) butter, cut into pieces
salt
freshly ground black pepper

Place the onion, 1¼ cups milk, breadcrumbs, nutmeg, butter and salt and pepper to taste in a medium bowl. Cover and cook for 5 minutes. Leave to stand, covered, for 15 minutes.

Remove the onion and add 2 more tablespoons of milk to thin, if necessary. Cook uncovered for 2 minutes longer, stirring halfway through cooking. Serve with roast chicken.

CRANBERRY RELISH

Makes about 1 cup Cooking time: 2 minutes
Microwave setting: Maximum (Full)

1 × 185 g jar cranberry sauce
grated rind of 1 orange
3 tablespoons orange juice
1 tablespoon brandy
1 tablespoon finely chopped glace ginger

Place the cranberry sauce and orange rind and juice in a bowl. Cover and cook for 2 minutes, stirring once.

Stir in the brandy and ginger. Serve hot or cold with roast turkey or ham.

TOMATO SAUCE

Makes about 2½ cups Cooking time: 13 minutes
Microwave setting: Maximum (Full)

30 g (1 oz) butter
1 onion, peeled and finely chopped
1 garlic clove, peeled and crushed
salt
1 teaspoon caster sugar
1 tablespoon chopped oregano
2 tablespoons tomato paste
2 tablespoons plain flour
600 g (1¼ lb) tomatoes, skinned and chopped
freshly ground black pepper
½ cup hot chicken stock

Place the butter, onion, garlic, salt, sugar, oregano and tomato paste in a large bowl. Cover and cook for 5 minutes.

Stir in the flour, tomatoes and pepper, then cover and cook for a further 5 minutes.

Stir in the hot stock. Cool the sauce slightly.

Pour into a blender and blend until smooth.

Sieve the sauce. Return to the bowl and reheat for 3 minutes before serving.

Serve with hamburgers, chops, sausages and fish.

Clockwise from top: Sauce Bearnaise; Bread sauce; Tomato sauce; Onion sauce; Curry sauce. Centre: Cranberry relish

ACKNOWLEDGEMENTS

Recipe Consultant: Jenny Webb
Editor and Food Consultant: Meg Thomason
Microwave adviser: Anne Arthur
Photography: Peter Myers, except for pp 2-3, 4-5, 28, 39, 45, 46: Charlie Stebbings; p 6: Theo Bergstrom
Photographic styling: Alison Williams and Paula Lovell
Preparation of food for photography: Michelle Thomson, Jennie Reekie and Margot Mason